DIVORCE

AN ESSENTIAL GUIDE

TO THE

INEVITABLE QUESTIONS

DIVORCE

AN ESSENTIAL GUIDE

TO THE

INEVITABLE QUESTIONS

L. B. THORNTON, ESQ.

TURNER

Turner Publishing Company

445 Park Avenue • 9th Floor
New York, NY 10022

200 4th Avenue North • Suite 950
Nashville, Tennessee 37219

www.turnerpublishing.com

Divorce: An Essential Guide to the Inevitable Questions

LEGAL DISCLAIMER:
"This publication is designed to provide accurate authoritative information in regard
to the subject matter covered. It is sold with the understanding that the publisher is not
engaged in rendering legal, accounting, or other professional service. If legal advice
or other expert assistance is required, the services of a competent professional person
should be sought." From a Declaration of Principles jointly adopted by a Committee of
American Bar Association and a Committee of Publishers.

The laws of each state regarding divorce are different and purchaser assumes
responsibility for adherence to all applicable laws of the state where they reside when
following the suggestions of this book.

Cover Design by Mike Penticost
Art Direction by Gina Binkley

Library of Congress Cataloging-in-Publication Data

Thornton, Linda B.
 Divorce : an essential guide to the inevitable questions / L. B. Thornton.
    p. cm.
 ISBN 978-1-59652-821-5
 1. Divorce. 2. Divorce--Economic aspects. 3. Divorce--Law and legislation. I. Title.
 HQ814.T477 2011
 306.89--dc22
                            2011003507

Printed in the United States of America
11 12 13 14 15 16 17—0 9 8 7 6 5 4 3 2 1

This book is also available in gift book format as
20 Things To Know About Divorce (978-1-59652-599-3)

To my husband Bobby, who believed in me, married me, divorced me, remarried me, and loved me for almost thirty years.

*"However often marriage is dissolved,
it remains indissoluble. Real divorce,
the divorce of heart and nerve and fiber, does not exist,
since there is no divorce from memory."*

~Virgilia Peterson

Contents

Introduction

Introduction

Hope is both the earliest and the most indispensable virtue inherent in the state of being alive. If life is to be sustained hope must remain, even where confidence is wounded, trust impaired.

—Erik H. Erikson

What courage you show. It took courage to open this book no matter what phase of divorce you are in. You are interested in getting a handle on this emotional, daunting process. Divorce is not for wimps, but neither is a bad marriage. This book was written to provide you with some basic things to know, ponder over, and work through, whether you are considering a divorce or are in the middle of one, or even if it's over. The information provided is based upon many years of law practice with people in all kinds of different situations. It is not a process book, but a book to provide you a way to be empowered during what may be one of the most emotional roller coasters of your life.

Because divorce is a state process, each state has its own requirements, deadlines, and processes. This is not a book specifically about those legal processes, but it will help you find the ones that apply to you. It will aim you in the right direction and provide some guideposts along the way. It will cover the generic issues encountered in the process— from the "we've grown apart" to addiction and physical and psychological abuse, and it provides insights into tough issues like child abuse, among others.

Every situation is different. All the people involved are different. This is not a one-size-fits-all book, but a book based on experience as a family lawyer and counselor involved in hundreds of divorce proceedings. It is not an all-encompassing treatise on divorce, nor does it provide legal advice. It is intended to provoke thought and provide necessary information about the divorce process.

My goal is to head you in the right direction, providing you with practical, plain-language answers to the questions you probably have on your mind right now. It will provide a solid foundation of information to prevent you from heading blindly into a process that is not for the faint of heart. I have designed the book to guide you to other people and information that can assist you in acquiring the knowledge you need to make informed decisions. Think of it as Divorce 101 or basic things you should know when divorce is on the horizon or in process. I provide information on topics such as how to find a lawyer, where to go to get financial help, how to decide if you need a marriage counselor, and how to begin finding one if you do. If this book causes you to think about issues and then talk about them with your spouse or others necessarily involved in your decision-making process, then it will have done its job.

Throughout the book are statistics as well as examples of situations taken from real cases. These thought-provoking examples provide you with an idea of what the process of divorce can be like, and they can also help you decide what is right for you and your family. None of the stories used as illustrations are taken from a specific family situation.

Divorce is similar to a boxing match in which the people in your corner have a stake, but the final outcome is determined by the two people in the ring battling it out: you and your spouse. Make no mistake, divorce is a battle. This book provides you with a strong starting point about how to find the right people to be on your team, but you will be the one who decides what is needed in your particular situation.

Even when both husband and wife amicably conclude their marriage, there are emotional outcomes for one party, or sometimes both, that impact the aftermath of divorce in unexpected ways. Therefore, there is a section to deal with the most common issues that arise after the divorce. Once the decision has been made to deliver your relationship to the hands of the court, your destiny becomes controlled by the state. Henceforth, you are at the mercy of the court and its decisions.

This book gives you a basic understanding of the terminology and general processes required to be informed. However, it does not offer legal advice and cannot be relied upon as providing legal advice. It will be important for you to obtain legal advice from a local family lawyer in your state who knows your specific situation, even if you ultimately decide to move forward on your own. Some things you need to know about finding a lawyer are included, as is a section on proceeding without a lawyer. You will read that each state has residency requirements, witness requirements, and other legal processes that must be followed.

The resource section is a nonexhaustive list of sources to obtain additional information on a variety of issues that will arise when you are contemplating or obtaining a divorce. It contains a list of helpful books, Web sites, organizations, and state agencies available to you—some free, some not free—to start your hunt for more in-depth discussions on issues raised in this book. Again, there is nothing magical or all-encompassing about these materials, but once you are armed with the right questions, they will provide a starting point for obtaining information to make decisions based on your particular circumstance and location.

An effort has been made to be gender neutral in the book where possible, except for purposes of readability and the fact that some situations are more common to men and others to women. Almost all circumstances discussed apply to both husband and wife, but they may apply differently in some cases, which I have identified for purposes of clarity.

The unique layout of the book is purposely designed to allow you to begin at any point, but because the process of dissolving a marriage is not necessarily a continuum, I urge you to read it all. All of the information found within these pages is valuable to your full understanding of what you can do at any time, whether divorce has begun or is over.

The first section provides the information to consider before any legal proceeding is begun but will also assist you even if you are in the middle of a divorce. The second section provides the information to consider during the legal proceeding itself, regardless of which spouse started the process, and the third section is focused on the issues that follow the legal proceeding. Parties can start a proceeding and stop it if they are in agreement. Divorce does not have to be a fatalistic process with a life of its own unless you allow it to be. You may be surprised at the number of people who remarry each other after a divorce, when the parties have "come to their senses."

Be informed and make wise choices. Divorce is a decision that will impact your life and the lives of all your family members for many years to come. Like marriage, divorce should not be entered into lightly.

Divorce is an extremely personal, fact-driven process. Nothing in this book is intended to provide specific instructions for a particular situation but rather to provide you with information—information to allow you to make more informed choices for yourself and your family. Only you can determine what applies to your particular situation and how you want to proceed.

No matter where you are at in the process—before, during, or after the divorce—it is my desire that this book will be a valuable asset to you as the process unfolds.

Best wishes,

L. B. Thornton

1
Can This Relationship Be Saved?

1

Can This Relationship Be Saved?

Loving someone is like caring for a garden,
love it too much or too little and it dies, but love it just right
and it will live forever.

—Anonymous

Choice. That is what this book is about. You and that special person in your life made the decision that you loved each other and wanted nothing more than to spend the rest of your lives with each other. You evidenced that choice by a decision to marry. Can you remember back to that time when you were both so full of excitement, joy, and passion that the thought of any separation, no matter how short, could barely be tolerated? The special day when the two of you wed was the highlight of your relationship.

Whether you married in a whirlwind with a short courtship or following a long engagement, the result was the
same: you became an officially married couple in the eyes
of the law. (As a side note, there are still some states that
recognize common-law marriage. If you are cohabitating,
it may be worth your time to check whether you are married according to your state's laws, even though you haven't
been through a ceremony.)

You woke every morning with the one person for whom
you waited your entire life. Your sole desire was for you
and that special someone to be blissfully happy together
forever. The two of you couldn't get enough time together,
and your desires and thoughts were all for each other, your
home, and possibly your children. Once, your special love
hung on to your every word, and you couldn't wait to hear
what your spouse would say next. Passions were high. At
the end of each day, you rushed into each other's waiting
and open arms—and now, you are reading this book. What
happened?

Perhaps you are reading this book for a friend, family member, or coworker, but if not, it is because you are
thinking about getting a divorce, have been served with divorce papers, or are wondering how you can change something in your Decree of Dissolution. If so, you have chosen
the right book.

It is my sincere desire that you and your loved one are
able to recover the love and enjoyment of the relationship you had in the early days of marriage, or improve and

strengthen your marriage even now. It is not too late. But if divorce is the decision you or your loved one have made, the real information provided here will guide you through the divorce process. Hopefully, it will help you move through the divorce without the total destruction of yourself, your loved one, your children, or your family along the way.

Divorce is not a solitary sport. It effects everyone around you: your spouse, your children (if any), your friends, family, extended family, and the friends and family of your spouse and anyone else who takes interest in you or loves you. All these relationships bring up issues you need to think about, such as adoption, including stepparent adoption, as you focus on making the right decision for yourself and your family. This brings me back to choice.

You chose to marry, and now you are contemplating ending that marriage. It will be important for you to carefully consider the reasons you think divorce may hold the answer for you: sometimes it does, and sometimes it doesn't.

Have you argued and one of you blurted out, "I want a divorce!" without even thinking about it? Did it scare you or set you to thinking? Either way, the thought is "out there," and now that the elephant is in the living room, you are looking for help. Be aware: it is time to proceed with extreme caution.

Some basic statistics

"Life is relationships; the rest is just details."

—GARY SMALLEY

The stark reality. Every day all over the world, people get married and they get divorced. In the United States alone, about 2.2 million people get married each year. But nowhere in the world do more marriages end in divorce than in the United States. According to the U.S. Census Bureau data for 2008 (published in 2009), one out of five marriages in the U.S. ends in divorce, and fewer people are getting married even though the population is increasing.

Statistically, your odds for staying married or getting a divorce are based on a number of things. Do you or your spouse have religious beliefs that prohibit or discourage divorce? Do you live in a city or in the country? In which state do you make your home? How old were you when you married? Have you ever been forced to have sex? Do you live in an area with a high level of male unemployment? What is your household income? Do you have children? All of these factors make a difference as to whether statistically your marriage will add to those numbers. However, these statistics are not set in stone. You can make a difference and beat the statistical odds.

Some states have higher divorce rates than others. They may provide easier access to the process, or divorce may be more socially acceptable in some states than in others.

For example, the U.S. Census has reported that for the past several years, Nevada has one of the highest divorce rates in the United States per 1,000 people, with Arkansas and Wyoming close behind. The lowest divorce rates in recent years were found in the District of Columbia, Massachusetts, and Pennsylvania. Some states like California do not provide data, so they are not included and perhaps could have higher or lower rates. This information is provided only to show that the state where you live can have an impact on whether your marriage will statistically remain intact. But I remind you, these are only general statistics and do not necessarily apply to your individual situation.

A report issued by the National Marriage Project at Rutgers University found that only 63 percent of American children grow up with both biological parents—the lowest figure in the Western world. The 2003 U.S. Census Bureau survey found that 43.7 percent of custodial mothers and 56.2 percent of custodial fathers were either separated or divorced. And in 2002, 7.8 million Americans paid about $40 billion in child or spousal support or some combination thereof (84 percent of the payers were men). These numbers are similar year after year.

Another report written in 1995 did a comprehensive, in-person study of over 10,000 women and found that certain situations create predicable marital and divorce probabilities. The full report examined eight outcomes of cohabitation and marriage based upon the examination of a wide variety of people and circumstances ("Cohabitation,

Marriage, Divorce, and Remarriage in the United States," Matthew D. Bramlett, Ph.D., and William D. Mosher, Ph.D., Division of Vital Statistics).

The researchers found that where a woman lives may be as important as other factors when it comes to maintaining a stable relationship. Other trends are based on racial makeup, belief in God, whether abuse has occurred, the amount of education of each spouse, and the incomes of the spouses.

Not surprisingly, those in lower income neighborhoods with less education and those who married young were the most likely to break up. This is particularly true for women of color (who are not Hispanic). But look out—those of you in the other brackets are not immune. This is particularly true if you have ever been forced to have sex.

Now that you have a better understanding of the statistical odds, we need to talk about what you can do right now to prevent yourself from becoming one of these statistics. So let's get started on taking the steps to see if this marriage can be saved.

Your relationship—where is it?

When you realize you want to spend the rest of your life with a person, you want the rest of your life to start as soon as possible.

—NORA EPHRON, WHEN HARRY MET SALLY

A little inventory. Let's begin at the beginning: you got married. The first thing to do now is to take an inventory of your relationship. Remove yourself from all distractions, turn off the TV, and find a quiet place where you can have some uninterrupted time to reflect on why you got married. Everyone has different reasons, but there is generally one thing that everyone who marries has in common: they believed they would be happier married than apart from one another. There is no one reason that will apply to everyone, but before you take steps to end your marriage, it is important to understand and think about why you got married in the first place and write those reasons down.

No matter how silly this seems, think back to how you felt on day you said "I do." Let your mind float freely and just write down the thoughts that come to mind. Was it because he made you laugh? Did she have a hot body? Whatever it was, you owe it to yourself to take some time here. Even if your divorce is under way or over, you will find this exercise helpful. In order to know where you want to be, it is important to spend some time thinking about how you got to this point in your relationship. If you are in a divorce now, this is particularly important because the process is emotionally devastating for most people.

Now, get a pen and paper. On the left half of the paper, write down everything that comes to mind that describes why you married. Don't wait—do it now while you are thinking about it. On the right side of the page, make a list of all the things that have changed in your relationship that make you unhappy. Again, write down everything you can think of that now makes you want a divorce, or makes you unhappy, that you would like to change. Does she have a lover? Does he? Is it finances? Whatever it is, ask yourself: If I had the power to make whatever change I desire in order to be happy, what would that change be? It may surprise you to see what you come up with. We spend a lot of time focusing on what others have done to us, but the real focus should be on us, what we have done or what we could do differently to improve the relationship.

Next, examine your two lists together. For each item on the list of why you married, do you have something that changed on the second list? Is that change something you control or can control? Are you seeking to change some behavior in your spouse? This is very common. Most of us see clearly the faults of others but do not as easily see those in ourselves. This is where it is important to be honest with yourself. Go back through the items on the right column and think about what you can do to correct these things you have identified and get your relationship back on track—back to where it was on the wedding day when you were sure you had made the right choice for the rest of your life.

You will find some things that are easily fixable and others that will take more time. Some may not be things that can be fixed at all. Do you spend a lot more time nagging and whining at your loved one than you did before? Maybe you are lying to your spouse, or perhaps you just don't even care enough to get dressed up anymore. These are common complaints from one spouse or the other. Some of these may seem trivial, but with enough small irritations, a relationship can be headed for divorce court.

Looking at your list, are all of these things fixable? Generally, unless addiction and abuse are present (we'll look at them in another chapter), with effort, many issues can be overcome and the relationship restored to its former passion. Contrary to popular belief, marriage does take work on the part of both spouses to keep it alive and fresh. Not the kind of work a job requires, but emotional work and sometimes physical too. Do you find you spend more time talking with your coworkers or friends than you do with your spouse? Is one partner using sex as a reward or a hammer? If so, ask yourself why, and then think about why this is happening. Is there something you can do to change it?

Successful marriages are built on a foundation of trust, mutual respect, and friendship. According to the Old Testament of the Bible, marriage was originally planned by God as a way for men and women not to be alone and to have a helpmate for life. Wives, are you being a helpmate? Are you a nag or a complainer? Do you treat your husband as a roommate? What about you husbands? Do you take your wife for granted? Do you treat your wife as your housekeeper? Do you show her the love you have for her?

Love and mutual respect are the basic pillars upon which marital trust is based. A wife needs to be secure in the knowledge she is loved, and a husband needs to know he has his wife's respect. Both husbands and wives need to be able to trust the other spouse. A woman generally responds to love and affection from her partner by returning that love and affection. A man generally responds to acknowledgement of his ability as a protector and the respect from his wife by showing her love.

Some of the most common reasons people give for wanting a divorce are "We've grown apart," "We aren't the same people anymore," "He takes me for granted," "She has a lover," "We are no longer in love," "We don't have sex," or "He is having a mid-life crisis and has left me." Whether you have been married for a year or less or twenty-five years or more makes no difference. What does make a difference is your choice. Do you want to save your marriage? If so, start today.

"Well," you say, "I've already been served," or "We are in the middle of a divorce already." You tell yourself, "I can't save my marriage, it's too late." Not so. Many times being served with divorce papers can actually be the wake-up call needed to save the marriage. It is amazing after receiving divorce papers how many spouses say, "I had no idea my spouse wanted a divorce." Is this you? Why?

Unfortunately, this is more common than you may realize. This is the case in which a spouse is so deep in denial about the shape of their relationship, having ignored all the signs of conflict or problems, that they would arrive at the lawyer's office and say, "Sure we have problems, but I had no idea it was as serious as this. I don't want a divorce, so why didn't he talk to me instead of filing for one?" These folks are almost incapable of recognizing their part in the problems of communication and often refuse to acknowledge the depth or seriousness of the issues or even that divorce was on the horizon. Even in cases of extreme denial, it still may not be too late, although help will be needed in the form of counseling, whether pastoral, marital, or psychological.

The starting point for repair of any relationship is the recognition that you may need help and that ultimately, men and women are different. They are wired differently. Their brains work differently. They think differently. They are created to accomplish different tasks, and sometimes these natural differences create friction in the marriage. I am not telling you one or the other is better, just that men and women are different, which means they think differently and approach relationships differently. There is a popular book, among many others on the market, called *Men Are from Mars, Women Are from Venus*, that attempts to provide insights into these differences. The Bible and other religious literature is also very helpful in looking at improving the relationships between husbands and wives.

Just one example of gender differences confirmed by psychological studies is that men speak about 20,000 words every day and women, about 80,000. How do you think that works if a man has been on the job all day and the woman at home all day with small children? It probably doesn't work very well. The husband comes in exhausted and is greeted by the wife who asks, "How was your day?" He says "Fine." The wife continues to ask questions, and the husband continues to give one-syllable answers. The wife becomes frustrated that her husband won't tell her what is going on, and he is aggravated because he thinks he has answered the questions satisfactorily and doesn't understand why she is still asking questions. Most men don't want all the details, and most women live for them. It's just one communication issue that those in successful marriages have learned to handle.

A woman's number-one need is love, and for a man, it is respect. Studies have found that although men are strong and perhaps even "macho" in some cultures, their egos are very fragile. A man can quickly slip into jealousy, anger, or frustration when he, as Rodney Dangerfield said, "gets no respect." Wives need to be sure to provide encouragement and respect so their husbands know they are respected. What can you do to reassure your husband that you do respect him? Do you compare him to your friend's husband or deride him because he has lost his job and can't find another? Do you still dress up for him when he comes in from work?

Just as women need to let their husbands know they are respected, men need to let their wives know they are still loved. An issue for many men to be aware of is that a work relationship can grow into something more as you and your coworkers share day-to-day experiences. This is a common trap for the married man who may enjoy the extra attention he is getting from that cute coworker. It is important to maintain a professional relationship with the women at work, particularly when they are encouraging more. It's okay to go out to lunch, but add some more folks to keep everything professional and limit the temptation that might otherwise exist. Also, men tend to be engaged in nights out with the guys, but make sure to have regular nights out with your wife too. Remember, women consider these acts of thoughtfulness as fulfilling their need to be loved.

Professional counseling can help you work through these issues and many others, so do yourself and your family a favor and find a good psychiatrist or counselor to help you weather these storms and return your relationship to what it was at the beginning. You can choose to make it happen.

If you are separated or if there is substantial animosity between you, counseling may not be possible right now. But even if you must take the action alone, I would encourage you to do so. One or both of you may not want to go, but this step can often help put the issues of your relationship in proper perspective. Also, many books have been written on how to improve your marriage, and bookstores and libraries are filled with material that can help you solve your marital problems if you are serious about taking action. But saving your marriage is something you and your spouse should work on together, if possible.

How can I find a good counselor?

If you attend a church, synagogue, or other place of worship, you can start there. Otherwise, you can see whether your state offers low- or no-cost counseling or mediation services to help you. Certainly there are the yellow pages, but you want to be sure you are able to get someone reputable. If possible, find a local lawyer in your area and ask for a referral to a good marriage counselor. Alternatively, most churches can provide you with a referral. There is also the Internet. See the resource section in this book for sources to help you get on the path of reconciliation with your spouse.

What if my spouse won't go with me?

That happens. But it shouldn't stop you from seeking counseling. It is something I always recommend because whether you divorce one another or not, counseling will help you keep your sanity during the divorce process and afterward. It is generally recommended that you not even contemplate entering another relationship or marriage until at least three years following a divorce. This is to allow enough time to pass to resolve the emotional baggage from the first relationship. Sometimes this baggage will also require counseling to work through. Counseling can help you restore your relationship or get through the emotional processes of the divorce so you can get on with your life. So if your spouse won't go, do it for yourself.

2
Till Debt or Abuse
Do Us Part

2

Till Debt or Abuse Do Us Part

Here's to man: he can afford anything he can get; here's to woman: she can afford anything she can get a man to get for her.

—GEORGE ADE, AMERICAN HUMORIST

A re finances stressing you out? In today's economic climate, your answer is probably yes. But whether economic times are good or bad, financial stress is tough on marriages. In fact, it is one of the most devastating issues couples face and is the most commonly cited reason for seeking a divorce.

Why would this be? Pressures from financial stress come from many sources, and no income bracket or social strata is immune. Whether both spouses are employed or not, the intense emotional issues caused from financial pressures can be almost unbearable if left unattended. Finances is a key area where spouses need to learn to work together. If you plan to cure specific financial problems in your marriage, it is also important to understand the underlying reasons for them.

Financial stress may be caused by whoever manages the money. Sometimes the most intense stressors occur when there are differences between you and your spouse on when to buy, what to buy, how to buy, and even whether something should be bought at all.

When either the husband or wife is stressed over job-related issues, it impacts the entire household. Studies have shown that children, regardless of age, will pick up on the tensions and add to the family dynamics by acting out, causing even more stress. Financial issues often create anxiety and depression that can lead to physical and mental issues that need to be attended to medically. Stress, depression, and frustration from out-of-control feelings can also lead to suicide and sometimes even criminal activity. Why does this happen?

Financial stress doesn't normally begin with a bang, but when left unattended, becomes like a snowball heading downhill, gathering more and more snow until it crushes everything in its path. If you or your spouse are thinking about divorce in the midst of turmoil caused by financial pressure, I would urge you to begin talking to each other about what concerns you. Discussing your finances together may seem like a normal thing; "Of course I will talk to my spouse about it," you may respond, but too frequently, that just doesn't happen. Surprisingly, few people seeking divorce actually talk through their financial issues before consulting an attorney, often because of the denial that accompanies finances. There may also be other issues, like abuse and drugs, that add to the financial pressures.

Financial issues can be driven by the emotional needs of a spouse to control, spend, or be stingy. When these needs are not compatible with income, or if the couple is living in debt from credit cards, it can often lead to arguments and discord. One spouse or the other may have a wrong understanding of just how much income is available for the family. When these kinds of issues aren't discussed, nothing will repair the problem.

Sometimes, one spouse may believe that their money is their own, and because they work hard for it, they should be able to spend it as they choose. Another may think, I make plenty of money, so there is no problem with my buying that boat, jewelry, or car without talking to the spouse that handles the finances. One of the biggest problems occurs when one spouse buys compulsively and fails to tell the other spouse, hiding or lying about what they buy. This will usually fail, but it doesn't stop the person from trying. These unattended financial issues often lead to divorce court.

Another common problem is one spouse taking out a credit card or loan without the other's knowledge. When that type of deceit is involved or when purchases are hidden from the husband or wife, the relationship deteriorates from a lack of trust and communication.

Left unchecked, these dysfunctional financial approaches—spending beyond income and racking up debt that is almost impossible to pay—will often lead to divorce court. Because finances heavily impact our lives, these unresolved issues will aggravate any other relationship or household issues. If there is no money, then there is no food, house, clothing, or car. If there is too much debt to be paid on the monthly income, creditor calls and collection letters will just add to the problem. Help yourself and your relationship by taking a hard look at this situation.

Even in good times, finances are often a huge part of domestic discord. If you or your spouse has lost employment, or if you've had an unexpected rash of expenses—like those in that old country song where the door is coming off the hinges, the roof is leaking, the window panes are broken, and life in general is falling apart—do not despair. Things can be done to help you get back on track. Believe it or not, just discussing your money problems with each other or a professional marital or debt counselor can help remove the pressure from your relationship. We will talk about finances in the context of divorce in later chapters, but here our focus is what can be done about them to relieve the relationship of pressure caused by debt.

When finances are a problem, there are usually communication failures involved and almost always a complete lack of understanding of the debt picture. Even the spouse handling the finances is often unable to face the reality of the problem and may have no idea just how much debt they are in or even how much money they bring home. This can be particularly true when one spouse is a tip earner. Many times, there is no real appreciation for how the tips add to the family income.

Finances are often considered the measuring stick of a man's ability as a provider. When a man is not able to meet the needs of his family, his self-worth is impacted, leading to a downward spiral of frustration, depression, and anger. This can lead to issues such as drinking or drugs or even pretending he is still employed. For women, financial issues create insecurity, and the lack of security strikes at a core need for security. If a spouse likes to spend, she may continue to spend even when there is no money. Perhaps it's the opposite problem. One of the spouses is so stingy they never want to spend a dime on anything even though money is plentiful. Both are problems. Both will lead to more and more arguments until communication shuts down completely.

The arguing and anger is usually an outward expression of an inner fear and, of course, is most often directed toward the people closest to us. This cycle of lack of self-worth, fear of not making ends meet, not being able to spend money, and outbursts of anger will often lead one party to be reluctant to go home. When confronted with this situation, the unhappy spouse often just doesn't go home and will find "some place" to be other than home. This may be a bar, a friend, or a lover. Depression fed by fear and anger can lead to suicide attempts by either the husband or wife or may lead to other destructive behavior, putting even more pressure on the relationship.

How to play the money game

The difference between divorce and legal separation is that legal separation gives a husband time to hide his money.

—JOHNNY CARSON

Communicating well, and often, is something each spouse can do. It may be hard to get started because of all the hurt and denial, but with help, it can be done. Your efforts will be rewarded in a number of ways. One is that trust will be restored between you and your spouse, trust that is usually degraded or nonexistent when financial trouble spirals out of control.

Money issues can be just as addictive and destructive as alcohol and drugs. They can also create the same kind of codependency issues as any other type of addiction and can be managed when they are acknowledged and not ignored. Often, if one spouse has a money addiction, the other spouse is codependent on money as well. It is for this reason that communication is so important to get out of the stranglehold of debt.

The other thing to watch for is the substitution of one addiction for another. This generally occurs when people with a drinking or drug addiction have successfully gotten their addiction under control but later find themselves involved in a new addiction, such as out-of-control spending, eating, or even sex.

Sometimes the issue is too much spending. Sometimes it is not enough spending. Sometimes it is just not enough money. It can even be too much money. Successful people who are money addicts can find themselves sabotaging the very success they seek, cyclically going from boom to bust and back to boom. Remember Willie Nelson? At the top of his career, he became well acquainted with his Internal Revenue Agent. What about Wayne Newton, who at his career pinnacle filed bankruptcy? Both men were making more a month than many people make in a year. If you are in financial hot water, you have plenty of company. Even well-known multimillionaires like Donald Trump and Richard Branson have filed bankruptcy.

To find out if bankruptcy is the right answer to relieve the stress of financial strain from your relationship, talk to a knowledgeable attorney or debt counselor. If you and your spouse are not working together to save your marriage, make sure you mention a potential divorce when you speak to your advisor. Divorce has an impact on how bankruptcy is handled. Get a solid understanding of your options, then talk with your spouse when possible to make the decision to declare bankruptcy together.

There are many resources to help you, ranging from credit counselors and bankruptcy lawyers to self-help books. Check out the resource section for some good places to start to dig out of the financial hole. It could very well save your marriage.

The color of pain and abuse

You can't stay married in a situation where you are afraid to go to sleep in case your wife might cut your throat.

—MIKE TYSON

If finances is the most common reason given for divorce, the most painful is when the relationship is abusive. Abuse comes in many different forms, the most common being physical, mental, emotional, and sexual. Like addictions, in whatever form it is found, abuse will destroy a marriage.

When there are issues of abuse, reconciliation may be more difficult depending on what form the abuse takes. Often a separation may be necessary while rehabilitation or counseling takes place. All family members may need counseling in some form, not just the abuser and the victim. In many cases of sexual abuse and incest, this is particularly true as other members of the family may be aiding the abuser or ignoring what they know, hoping it will just stop. However, an abuser may not be able to stop his behavior without help. The criminal nature of some abuse will cause other complications for the family but can sometimes be the wake-up call needed to get the help to begin the healing and recovery process.

Abuse leads to emotional and sometimes physical scars of family members that can last a lifetime. It can even lead to death. Take the situation of Edwin Valero and his wife Jennifer. Valero, a former boxing champion with twenty-seven straight knockouts, was found in his jail cell hanged by his clothes on April 19, 2010. He had been incarcerated for stabbing his wife to death in their hotel room. Jennifer was also harassed by him in March while she was in the hospital being treated for injuries from a prior assault. Valero also harassed the hospital staff who with Jennifer charged him with harassment. This may be the trigger that led him to kill her, but no one will ever know. What we do know is that Valero suffered from depression and an addiction to alcohol and drugs. With incidents of prior abuse, these made a deadly combination. The couple's two children now have no parents.

If you have any of these issues in your relationship, get help now before it is too late. Most women are abused by someone they know, often a spouse or another loved one. The emotional scars will impact all of the victim's relationships, and the abuser's also. This type of dysfunctionality may be connected with other addictions or usage of drugs (legal or illegal) and alcohol. But abuse is usually a control issue, so the abuser may not misuse drugs or alcohol.

Many abusers were themselves abused as children, and

although they hated what was happening to them, they grow up and treat their family members the way they were treated or the way they saw their parents act. Because of the physical danger caused by this type of abuse, divorce or legal separation may be necessary for the family's safety.

Whether you are the abused or the abuser, there are options to help you overcome the emotional scars and deal with the frustration or powerlessness that keeps you in the abuse cycle. Like Jennifer, women in particular find it difficult to leave the abuser, even when they know the situation is dysfunctional. They often file paperwork to have the abuser arrested or removed from the home, only to change their minds and withdraw it. Abusers may claim remorse, but they will seldom stop their behavior on their own.

Abusers come in all shapes, sizes, and genders, including male, female, and even children. It is not uncommon for those in this situation to deny the abuse. Many victims are embarrassed and don't want others to know what is going on behind closed doors. Child victims are often told by the abuser not to tell anyone, and out of fear or due to threats, they don't. Abuse is about control. It may appear to be about rage, anger, or jealousy, but those are the ways it manifests itself. If you see symptoms of abuse, if you are physically hurt, or if anyone strikes or hits you, get help for both of you.

Insecurity from not knowing what to do if the abuser leaves coupled with the fear of the unknown can keep a codependent spouse from filing for divorce. The spouse may also be reluctant to find a safe place to go. If this is you, please locate a local safe house. Check the resources in this book for places to begin. Don't let fear keep you from taking action to protect yourself and your children.

Many addicts or abusers are married to rescuers or facilitators. In these situations, the addict may get help and resolve their addiction problem, only to find the marriage falls apart because the codependent facilitator or rescuer did not get help with them. They often feel they are no longer needed and frequently find they have no identity once the addict is no longer an addict. The movie *Days of Wine and Roses* with Lee Remick and Jack Lemmon clearly depicts the pain and love of an alcoholic married to another alcoholic. The husband finds his way, but he can no longer live with his alcoholic wife. Sometimes we can recognize that someone else has a problem, but it is hard to change ourselves.

Marriage requires work from both partners. No one can do it alone. Marriage is a team sport in which the parties must be able to handle the day-to-day issues of life and show that they care about each other. No matter how monetarily successful you are, abuse can still happen. Ike and Tina Turner and Whitney Houston and her husband Bobby Brown had successful music careers and in public appeared to have everything. But no amount of success could change the abusers they lived with.

Statistics show that marriages built on love, trust, commitment to one another, and mutual respect last.

When any one of these factors is missing, the relationship suffers.

Where can I find help?

Several resources are available to help those in an abusive relationship. Many charitable organizations like the Salvation Army and churches can provide you with assistance. These organizations have shelters or are connected with safe houses or shelters for these situations.

Most cities and communities also have safe havens or women's shelters, generally listed without a street address and only with a phone number. They are usually designed for immediate, short-term assistance, but they may be able to direct you to the resources you require. Some will not allow children except for the first night. They will all usually be able to put you in touch with a group or advocate or someone else who can help you.

Because it is less common, there are fewer options for battered men. In most areas, the Salvation Army and YMCA may provide locations where men can stay, or they may be able to help you find appropriate resources.

Some organizations offer funds for you to get assistance obtaining a place to stay while you get help, and you may be able to take advantage of state-sponsored programs for battered spouses and children.

A multitude of self-help books, counselors, and psychologists can also provide assistance. Many states provide help through the court system. Some of the best programs are the twelve-step programs like Alcoholics Anonymous and Al-Anon, which helps the nonaddicted, codependent spouse.

Your local law library, health and welfare (social services) department, and sheriff or police department may be able to provide answers to questions and direct you to the right place to get help. Your public defender or prosecutor may also be able to provide useful guidance. If your state has a family court or mediation center, they, too, may provide information for you.

If you are afraid for yourself or your family because your spouse has threatened to hurt himself or others, you may be able to force the abuser into a detoxification or psychiatric facility for short-term evaluation under your state's law. This can sometimes be initiated by the police in response to a 9-1-1 call, depending on where you live. It may require legal assistance.

The key here is to recognize you need help and to get it. None of the programs for abuse works well if there is no acknowledgement of a problem.

3
Come See My New Red Ferrari

3
Come See My New Red Ferrari

"The mass of men lead lives of quiet desperation."

—Henry David Thoreau

There are specific years in a marriage that seem destined for divorce. Most common are year one, year seven, and year twenty. These are crisis years for relationships for different reasons. Year one is usually about incompatibility and selfishness. The discovery of each other becomes the discovery that that special loved one never picks up after themselves or can't hold or get a job. If a relationship survives the first-year anniversary, the next problem years are seven and ten years, explored in the Marilyn Monroe movie *The Seven Year Itch.* As in the movie, the husband or wife may find themselves facing an unexpected opportunity and due to curiosity, boredom, or just because they can, avail themselves of the chance. The next thing you know, the marriage is in trouble.

There is usually a fairly good chance the marriage, if it survives these early years, will be fine. But the next common time for problems is when the children grow up. Empty nesters, as they are known, are now without children for the first time in eighteen to twenty-five years or so. Some couples find they have lost sight of each other without the focus on their children. When these couples rediscover each other and find they no longer have anything in common, rather than attempt to rekindle the romance they had before, they head to divorce court.

The day-to-day irritations that bring people in the early years of marriage to seek divorce are not what causes the big distress in the midlife, long-term marriage. Spouses who try to ignore things that drive them nuts will often end up in a law office, when talking about these things with their spouse would have gone a long way toward restoring the marital bliss most couples seek.

Why is a midlife crisis so hard to get through?

A wife will say, "We were happy and comfortable. We just got to the place where we could enjoy life, and then after twenty-five years of marriage, he's changed." This scenario is a lot more common than one may expect. In fact, this group is fast becoming the group most likely to seek a divorce. Why would many long-term marriage partners all of sudden decide to divorce? Is it really so surprising? Most of the time when a long-term marriage is failing, one spouse will be hiding their head in the sand, refusing to see the signs before them. Often, the unhappy spouse has been telegraphing his or her feelings for years before reaching the point where he or she throws in the towel and files the divorce papers. Why are the signs not seen? What are the signs? Why does the unsuspecting spouse who was happy feel betrayed?

According to psychologists, human beings operate in very predictable ways. This predictability applies to marriage as well. In her book *Passages,* Gail Sheehy deals with the midlife crisis as one such predictable experience of human beings. She theorizes that in each decade of life, people go through similar phases that can be predicted. Usually the midlife crisis is thought of as something that affects only men, but Sheehy believes midlife crisis is something all human beings experience at different levels.

Now, the midlife crisis (not necessarily the same as middle age) is such a well-known, common phenomena that movies and books of all kinds use as the basis for their plots. It can be seen in the "Trophy Wife" syndrome. Who can forget Anna Nicole Smith and her ninety-year-old millionaire husband? He left her all his money as his spouse, and the children from his prior marriage took her to court. Examining these and similar phenomena was the stuff from which Gail Sheehy made her career.

Midlife is one of those periods of time in a man's or woman's life that can turn a long, stable marriage upside down. One day the husband begins to dress differently, becomes concerned about his weight and hairline, and comes home in a new red convertible. He's pushing for excitement, and you think he's lost his mind. Well, hang on to your hat; you are about to start a very bumpy ride. If you can weather the storm to come, you may be able to ride it out until he returns to himself and recognizes the comfort and satisfaction he had in your relationship and prevent yourself from becoming another statistic.

Many women have been blindsided in this way. They ignored the signs of their peril. Is it only men who go through this? No, but it is more frequently seen in men. Men who are bored, feel that life no longer presents a challenge because they are at the top of their career, or feel that life may be passing them by and that they have lost out on their dreams of youth.

Before he quits his job and runs off to Tahiti to fulfill his lifelong dream, you may be able to help make some smaller adjustments like taking ballroom dancing lessons, joining a gym, or doing something to move out of the boredom that seems to be a part of the malaise. Left to its own devices, a midlife crisis can make you find yourself center stage in the drama that turns your solid life upside down. No matter how successful a person is, there is nothing like the midlife crisis to make a spouse feel inadequate, looking into the bathroom mirror thinking, "Is that all there is?" It may even lead to clinical depression. Some symptoms are subtle and some are not, but this is a time to be alert and ready to make small changes to stop the larger ones from taking over.

This phase of life may leave your man with a sense of overwhelming paralysis, or the sense of being stuck and not knowing what to do about it. All of these feelings can be overcome if they are not ignored, and life can return to normal.

It is certainly easier to deal with these needs for change before the fantasy of a new wife or husband or having a new woman or man in life becomes a reality. Keep in mind there are many ways to address this, but the most important is not to ignore these feelings of life having passed by. This is not generally something women experience in the same way, but it can happen. If you are in a long-term marriage, I urge you to find a way to spice up the humdrum and everyday sameness that is often a part of this process. If you do, you may save your marriage.

Now that we know about it, what do we do?

Pain is God's megaphone to wake us up to bring us to Him.

—C. S. LEWIS

A midlife crisis is often the attempt to restart life to better fit a person's heart. We get so busy with work and life and making personal commitments that the overwhelming feelings and inner conflict are not easy to resolve by ourselves. These conflicts and feelings often cause a person struggling with the contradictions of life to act confused or lost while they try to make sense of how they feel and the changes they are going through. Resilience is the name of the game now. Change is the remedy, but controlled change—not throwing an entire lifetime away.

Are you or your spouse making changes just to make them but without a plan? Are you bored with life and looking for excitement? Are there changes in your sexual relationship? (Either more or less interest can be a concern.) Do either of you have a new interest in your physical appearance or clothes, or an obsession with the mirror? Do either of you express things like, "Life has passed me by," or "I feel trapped"? Is he remembering his glory days of college or high school? Perhaps one of you are talking about a series of "what if" scenarios. Is he drinking more and sleeping less? Is there just a sense of general dissatisfaction with where she is and what she is doing? How about depression? Perhaps there is an obsession with his mortality, usually seen when good friends have died, and he turns his thoughts to his own mortality. Because of all the information in the marketplace about midlife crisis, your spouse may even claim, "Maybe it's a midlife crisis."

If you are in that middle-life situation and have been married twenty or more years, keep a close watch on changes in your relationship and make sure you and your spouse talk about them. Don't wait until he finds that soft shoulder at his office, or until she is making secret phone calls. Your spouse may not want to talk or may not even be able to put their finger on why they feel like do. Take action. Do it in small ways in order that you may forestall the more abrupt ones like waking up to the new Porsche in the driveway (that you can't afford). You could wake up and find he has quit his job as CEO and has bought tickets for missionary work in Africa or Mexico or some other country.

If your husband's shirt smells of perfume, if you find lipstick on his collar, or if strange women call and hang up, then it is likely the divorce court will be his next move. This situation will usually require marriage counseling to keep your marriage together. Even so, this is not the end unless you and he choose to allow it to end.

If you are in this place, there are many books that have been written on how to improve your marriage. Bookstores and libraries are filled with materials that can help you solve the problem in your marriage if you are serious about taking action, but it is something you and your spouse should work on together.

Check the resource section in the back of the book to begin looking for counseling or Web sites that can provide you with ways to get through the midlife crisis and move on to old age together, marriage intact.

4
What About the Children?

4
What About the Children?

The first half of our lives is ruined by our parents;
and the second half by our children.

—Clarence Darrow

Children: blessing or curse?

Children are a gift from God. Many women believe they are incomplete without a child, and many men believe children are necessary to carry on the family name or business. Children can also be seen as problems. Some couples have them and wish they didn't, and others don't have them and wish they did. They can be a challenge to the best of marriages, but they can also create added turmoil that drives wedges between the parents when the mom and dad have different religious beliefs and certainly when they have different methods of child-rearing.

Before I got married I had six theories about bringing up children; now I have six children, and no theories.

—LORD ROCHESTER, ENGLISH POET

Differences in child-rearing practices can cause huge strife in a marriage and if not addressed, can lead to divorce. Why? If one parent is lenient and one is a strict disciplinarian, the lack of consistency will cause the children to play the parents against each other. Children are very smart about these things. Sometimes one parent will favor one child and the other parent a different child. This favoritism is recognized by the children and can often lead to marital problems between the parents. If the differences are serious enough, the ensuing arguments and frustrations can create tension that makes it hard for the parents to stay together unless one totally gives in to the other. And then new problems arise. These are not easy fixes, and no one can say whether one method is better than another, but if mom and dad open a door to dissent, the children will take advantage of it. It's just human nature.

The differences in philosophy may also be accompanied by differences in other areas. If dad is a doctor or lawyer or wanted to be one, there may be pressure on the child to do the same. When one parent pushes one way and the child another, parents can take sides, and this, too, can cause an otherwise happy couple to consider divorce as an answer.

Children may be closer to one parent or the other depending on their age and sex. Girls are generally closer to their moms until their teen years and boys to their fathers. Both parents are important for the proper development of the children, who learn what they live. We all know the old saying, "Do as I say, not as I do," but children learn to do what they see. No amount of coaxing will cause them to quit fighting if they see their parents fighting.

The stress of rebellious children, ill children, unwanted children, stepchildren, or even adopted children (especially when natural children follow) can all lead to divorce. It isn't that the children are bad or cause the issues; it is generally the way the parents react to what the children say or do that causes the stress. It is most commonly seen when parents feel trapped by their children. This sense of frustration in both men and women sometimes leads one parent to abandon the home, leaving the responsibility of the home and children to the remaining parent. This may occur when there are unresolved or undiscussed issues and friction between the parents.

One of the most difficult situations for the children is when one parent uses them as weapons against the other parent. This is damaging for all concerned, and appropriate counseling should be obtained to assist in changing the behavior. But what about couples who unexpectedly have children with disabilities or expect one child and get three or more? With the status of today's medical treatments, unwanted children can be aborted, but that too can bring problems of guilt or remorse that take their toll on the psyche of the marriage partners.

If your relationship problems are primarily due to your children, get help. If you are housebound because of a special-needs child in the home, you may become cranky or feel that your spouse takes you for granted. If there are financial problems due to medical or other costs of rearing the children no matter what their circumstances, then talk to one of the many different charity organizations or places of worship available in your community to see what help they can provide. Some groups and services have programs that allow you and your spouse time to be alone while they take care of the children.

If a wife or husband begrudges the time children spend with their mom or dad, or if dad wants all of mom's attention for himself (or vice versa) despite the needs of the children, the tension created often leads to arguments and frustration, which, if not resolved, can lead to divorce. The reverse is also true when one or both parents neglect the children. When this occurs, each party in the divorce often describes unruly children and attributes the misbehavior to the other parent.

Though they are sometimes able to do it regardless of their parental nurturing, children require two loving parents to grow into successful adults. But because we are not perfect people and because children are not miniatures of their parents but individuals in their own right, they can often be found at the center of marital issues. Issues stemming from parenting may sometimes be ancillary to other problems of the parents.

Depending on the status of the relationship, children can bring parents closer or move them farther apart. If a parent favors one of the children, it creates additional stress on all aspects of the family. No, this is not a book on child-rearing practices, but this discussion allows you to examine yourself and your family to see whether there are any changes that can be made to reduce pressure and thereby improve your family and marriage.

When a mom is too wrapped up in the children to pay attention to the dad, the relationship tends to deteriorate. There is on occasion such dysfunction in a family—characterized by abuse, addiction, and anger—that it can actually lead to crime. It might even be the children who are committing crimes if they are running with a wild crowd, in a gang, or doing drugs. These may be wake-up calls, but they may also be too late. Only you can know how the family interactions play out. Often, we are blind to our own faults, so I encourage you to take a hard look at these issues if they exist in order to find the right source of help to save the marriage, the children, and all the family relationships.

If one parent or even both have focused their full attention on the children, when the kids leave home the parents find they haven't had a conversation with one another for years and feel they have nothing in common anymore. One of the only things that can repair the relationship at this point is trying to reacquaint yourselves and making a commitment to one another.

A new phenomenon in today's society is kids who fail to leave home and start their own lives, or even married children moving in with their parents. Although extended family arrangements like this can be good, they can again bring stress and put the parents' marital relationship at risk. This is seen most often when one spouse is particularly stressed over the circumstance, especially if they were looking forward to a time of retirement and freedom but are still providing for their grown children or are now involved in rearing grandchildren.

An important step in working through all these situations is to examine your feelings and talk to your spouse about how they feel so that changes can be made to move the two of you to a place of compromise. No matter how hard it may be and how long it may take, it is worth it to try to save the marriage. The problems you face will determine the action you will need to take, but the first thing is to figure out whether you and your spouse can make the changes on your own or whether you need professional attention.

5
Three's a Crowd

5
Three's a Crowd

Eighty percent of married men cheat in America. The rest cheat in Europe.

—Jackie Mason

I'm sure you've heard the old saying, "A man chases a woman until she catches him." Women are typically seeking security in their relationships with men. They want a comfortable home to rear their children and a man they can depend on to bring home the bacon. Men, on the other hand, typically want to be respected. For women, love may be expressed when the husband holds or cuddles with them and no intercourse occurs, while men typically seek sexual relations as their expression of love. What this means is that husbands may have to learn that not every action of hugging or kissing should lead to the bedroom, and for women it is important to understand that their husband needs to be sexually fulfilled. A wise man once wrote that a husband's body belongs to his wife and a wife's body to her husband. If you keep that in mind, many of the hurtful things done in the name of love can be stopped.

Remember back to the time of courtship. Did you ever greet your loved one with curlers in your hair or wearing a sloppy robe and slippers? Did you sit on the couch in your underwear with a beer in one hand and a remote in the other? Probably not, but situations such as these happen so often in marriage that they have become the basis for television sitcoms. How often do the two of you date each other anymore? It is an important part of relationships to do things together. The date doesn't have to be expensive and may be nothing more than a picnic or walk in the park, but it needs to be something you enjoy doing together. If not, the relationship is ripe for a wandering eye to look to greener pastures.

Maybe you are just experiencing "the grass is greener" syndrome. Do you compare your relationship with what you hear from your coworkers and friends about their relationships? Stop! Focus on your relationship and remember that no matter how similar their circumstances are to yours, there is generally something you can't see from the outside. Also keep in mind that all day a husband is surrounded by women at work who may be professional in their appearance, and the same is true for the wife who works outside

the home, with all those men around her flirting at the water cooler. Considering this, if you are "curler mama" or
"couch-potato-remote man," there could be problems.

Psychologists have confirmed that the number-one
need of women is to feel they are loved. Your husband fulfilled this during the courtship, and once you were married, he promptly stopped taking you on dates and doing
those little things that showed you he was interested and let
you know he loved you. As the old joke goes, he felt like he
told you once and that nothing had changed, so there was
no reason to say it again. Little did he know that for you
as a woman, it was important for him to tell you that you
are loved, and for him to show you by letting you know he
appreciates you. From your point of view as a woman, you
think, "It doesn't seem to be so much to ask, does it?"

Well, maybe not for you, but it's just not how all men
are wired. Sometimes they need to be encouraged to be
romantic. Both husbands and wives often find they have
different ideas about what it takes to make the relationship
work. How often have you enjoyed a good game of football
or his favorite sport since you married? Weren't you the one
that went with him to every game before you got married?
He loves being outdoors, but are you still that fun-loving
woman who acted like you enjoyed it? Do you as a husband
still snuggle with her and watch those chick flicks together
like you used to? Check out some of the books on restoring
the sizzle in your relationship to get plenty of ideas.

Talk to your religious advisor or a marriage counselor and start to make changes in yourself to restore your relationship. How you handle the issue of your spouse having an affair or mistress or even a one-night stand may be the difference between a continuing marriage and a divorce.

Marriage requires two people to work to become one. One person cannot do all the work. If this is your situation, your spouse may seek someone else to fulfill the needs that you should be fulfilling within the marriage.

6
Considerations of a Religious Nature

6

Considerations of a Religious Nature

Love is patient; love is kind.
Love does not envy;
is not boastful; is not conceited;
does not act improperly; is not selfish;
is not provoked; does not keep a record of wrongs;
finds no joy in unrighteousness,
but rejoices in all truth;
bears all things, believes all things,
hopes all things, endures all things.
Love never ends.

—I Corinthians 13:4–8a (New King James)

This passage from the Bible is arguably one of the best definitions of love ever written. It speaks to the issues of human relationships that are most often found at the root of dissension in marriage. Though not easy, if these things are practiced, marriages can be restored. Why? Often impatience, anger, envy, stinginess, lack of kindness, or abuse of one kind or another are the key issues found in relationships that don't succeed. Each of the previous chapters of this book has looked at these most cited causes of divorce and marital discord.

How does divorce work with my belief system?

If you are in a place where you believe your marriage is worth saving and you are struggling to know what to do about it, then read this passage again. Think about what it means and how you can begin to take steps to put these ideas into practice on a daily basis. This particular approach has done more to save marriages from the divorce court than almost any other single thing I know. If you combine your application of these traits with sincerity and seek counseling (even if you have to go alone), you may find that your relationship can be turned around.

Perhaps you are not religious or have a belief system that is not structured. Either way, each culture, social group, or world religion has a viewpoint on divorce. Most religions will allow it with little or no formality. But because men and women are naturally inclined to be together, regardless of religious preference, divorce is not the optimum plan.

Have you ever spoken to someone in a successful long-term marriage of thirty or more years after they have lost their life partner to death? Many times you will hear the survivor say, "I feel as if part of me is gone," or "I have lost my identity." Equal partners in a good marriage will grow more alike over the years, and when death comes for one spouse, in many instances, the other spouse is not far behind. Why does this happen? The two really have become one, particularly when couples have lived fifty or sixty years of their lives together. With the availability of divorce and the lack of social stigma, our society is often amazed that people can be together in a loving relationship for ten years, much less fifty or sixty.

Prior to the societal love fest of the 1960s, long-term marriage was more the norm than we see today. People before the 60s love-in, sit-in, drop-out movements were more stable in their relationships. Were they perfect? No. Did they cheat? Yes, but most of them found ways to live together without the pain and anguish of divorce. Today, we have a disposable paper-plate mentality that affects our relationships. You may think, It's not worth the effort to try to restore or save my relationship when I can find someone else who is more in tune with me.

This "grass-is-greener" syndrome may or may not work. As Erma Bombeck wrote, the grass may be greener because it's over the septic tank. An old comedy dealing with this issue, *Boys' Night Out,* played on the fantasy of some men to have beautiful mistresses who would meet their every desire, but the men finally recognized that they really loved their wives. This dream of truly loving your spouse can be fulfilled at home with the right efforts and mindset.

Today, a new phenomenon has sprung up: the "cougar," a middle-aged or older woman out for a "good time" with a younger man. The movie *The Graduate* explores this issue, and today, the cougar relationship is being seen more and more often. These new huntresses, often divorcees, have determined that this is the way to deal with reentering the dating game after long-term relationships end, but it can be a dangerous game.

Whether married six months or six years or more, many people fail to get to know why their relationship failed in the first place and bring all the emotional, destructive habits from their past into the new relationship. Then the cycle begins again. Not clearing up personal issues from your past that influenced the breakup of your marriage may prevent you from entering into a new successful marriage.

Can I get an annulment?

When parties recognize that their marriage was a mistake from the beginning and wish to annul the marriage, it can be done in most states under certain very limited circumstances. It is not the same as obtaining a divorce, although it can be either contested or uncontested. Check with a lawyer in your state for details on what is cause for annulment and how one can be obtained.

Short-term (one or two days) unconsummated marriages (main issue in most annulments) are, generally speaking, the easiest marriages to get annulled. Incapacity such as not knowing you were getting married due to being drunk or under the influence of drugs can be another reason for annulment in most states.

Some religious groups have their own rules about divorce that must be followed in addition to those of the state in which they reside. Orthodox Jews, Catholics, and Muslims, to name a few, have their own criteria for divorce or annulment of marriages. Most notably, Catholics have sought and obtained special dispensation from the Pope for divorces or annulments.

It is normally difficult to have a marriage annulled after children have been born because there are other consequences to be addressed, such as paternity and support. You should still ask your local lawyer to see if annulment is available to you. This process is extremely fact-driven, so it is important to discuss if it is what you choose to do.

7
Opening the Door of the Courtroom

7

Opening the Door of
the Courtroom

*Divorce is a declaration of independence with only
two signers.*

—Gerald Lieberman

Do I need a lawyer, or can I use the simplified divorce package from the state?

Do-it-yourself divorces are available in most states and are primarily structured for people who have no property or children or have a completed, signed settlement agreement for the divorce. If this is you, then you can do it yourself. Generally, the simplified divorce processes do not provide for child support or alimony. If you are in need of these types of monies, then this process won't be for you.

Be aware that the do-it-yourself process is designed for people who are in total agreement about their breakup. Even one item of disagreement will prevent a do-it-yourself process in most states where it is available. In some states parties with children are not allowed to file for divorce without counsel, even if they are in complete agreement on everything. Others will not allow people who own property to file for a divorce on their own. If you are in agreement and have no children or property, or just don't want to have the expense of a lawyer, then you may be able to file what is called a "pro se" pleading, but the simplified forms offered by the state will not be available to you. Knowing what processes are available where you live will be important in deciding whether you want to do it alone.

Another option is to use the initial consultation with your lawyer to get legal advice. Many family lawyers will provide a free half-hour consultation or low-cost consultation that you can use to get information and answers, whether you hire the lawyer or not. (See the chapter on getting an attorney and the resource section for more on this.)

There is a whole chapter later in this book on changes to the pro se or normal, lawyer-handled divorce decree. If you are considering this approach, be sure to read on so you can be informed about what you may be giving up before you decide whether to go through with it alone. For example, some states will not allow a do-it-yourself decree of divorce to be modified.

If you decide this is the approach for you, step one is to get the state forms. They are usually purchased from the Clerk of Court in the county where you reside. The package will normally include the filing fee for the divorce, and there is no need to serve the papers on your spouse because you are both going to sign the papers in the package and attend the court proceeding together. It can be a fairly painless process from a procedural standpoint, but the emotional issues will still be present, even if they don't surface at the time of the divorce.

Going pro se

If you just don't want to use a lawyer and aren't eligible for the simplified process, then you can be your own attorney. You will still have to follow the court procedures and do the same things a lawyer can do for you. Forms can be purchased online, and your local law library can provide guidance for you. It is important to keep in mind that there are probably areas of the law you won't understand and may overlook by doing it yourself. If you choose this direction, I remind you of the old adage: "The lawyer who handles his own matter has a fool for a client." This applies doubly for the non-lawyer handling his own matter. Having said that, you can talk with lawyers using their free or low-cost consultation or even by arranging to pay for their advice by the hour. This may help, but again, I caution against this approach.

One lawyer, one divorce

Just another of our many disagreements. He wants a no-fault divorce, whereas I would prefer to have the bastard crucified.

—J. B. Handlesman

The better alternative may be for you and your spouse to lay out your agreements using a bullet-point approach. Then one of you can hire a lawyer to proceed in an uncontested manner. This lawyer will prepare a settlement agreement for his client, and then both of you will sign the agreement. In this approach, only one of you will be represented, but this can be a very workable solution if both you and your wife are looking for a less costly approach to divorce and are able to work together amicably. The more resigned the other party is to obtain a divorce, the more potential there is for this to be effective.

If you and your spouse use this approach, the nonrepresented spouse should then use a one half-hour consultation with a different family lawyer to have the settlement agreement reviewed on their behalf. By doing this, the nonrepresented spouse can gain a sense of comfort about some of the legalese found in these agreements. It will also provide an opportunity for the nonrepresented spouse to find out whether the bullet-point agreements properly reflect each party's decisions and are appropriate, and whether the agreement has any adverse items that were unexpected. The spouse may find that they have agreed to do, pay, or give more than their fair share. This discussion will be important to gain a thorough understanding of the agreement before it is signed and to find out about issues you need to discuss with your spouse before the divorce is completed.

If these issues are serious enough, both of you may need your own lawyers, and the divorce may then move into the contested column. But the only way you will know is to get that review. If these issues can be resolved, the agreement can be changed before the divorce is final, and the outcome of the proceeding will be more satisfactory to both of you. Most attorneys who draft a settlement agreement will be willing to make the changes if you as the client and your spouse agree to them. If not, then each of you will need to prepare to get your attorneys and battle it out.

If you are thinking of going through with the divorce process alone, my recommended direction is this latter method of hiring only one lawyer, with the other party having the agreement reviewed by another lawyer. Although you have a right to represent yourself pro se and be your own lawyer, I would not recommend it because there are too many pitfalls for the layman in the courtroom, with technicalities and details that may become snares for you. Remember, the judge will require you to follow the same procedures as a lawyer. If you miss a deadline, fail to file a proper response, or forget to properly serve your answer or other documents, you can be prevented from participating in the proceeding. This can be a very troublesome outcome for you.

8
Hiring an Attorney

8
Hiring an Attorney

A lawyer is never entirely comfortable with a friendly divorce, any more than a good mortician wants to finish his job and then have the patient sit up on the table.

—*TIME* MAGAZINE

As in any business, lawyers are best found by word of mouth from friends, coworkers, and others who have had experience with them. This familiarity will provide you with the benefit of their outcomes and feelings about how their divorce was handled. It is important to keep in mind, however, that not every situation is the same, and even if your friend had a great outcome, there is no guarantee yours will be the same. It does mean that you will know something about the attorney.

Choosing an attorney is an important part of the divorce process. You need to be sure you are able to work with the attorney. If you are emotionally distraught and not thinking clearly because you are upset, angry, depressed, or have been surprised by being served, then you will need an attorney who is able to handle your emotionality and help you understand the process and what you need to do. This is a lot harder than it seems because clients and lawyers all approach the process differently. There is also a need for trust on both sides: the lawyer needs to know he can count on you to provide the information needed to properly do the job you expect, and the client needs to know the lawyer will look out for their best interest in an emotional and difficult time when many clients are not really at their best.

When your friends cannot help you with recommendations, or if you don't like the ones they recommend for whatever reason, you can contact the State Bar Association where you live. Almost every State Bar Association and even some County Bar Associations have lawyer referral services.

Most larger libraries have a set of books called the Martindale Hubbell that include listings of all licensed attorneys near you. This multivolume set lists basic areas of practice and other information, including a rating on each lawyer's ability and ethics. The top rating for attorneys is shown as AV rating, which is the one you need to look for. The lawyer cannot control the ratings—they are done by the Martindale Hubbell Corporation itself. Lawyers know the good rating makes a difference and it should make a difference to you.

The Martindale Hubbell is also online if you don't want to go to a library or if one isn't available to you. In the resource section are links and Web sites to contact referral's services as well as other avenues to get a good lawyer for your case.

Doing your due diligence: tips for finding someone who works for you

Once you have settled on some names of attorneys, whether from the yellow pages, referrals from friends, or a bar association, there are questions you need to ask each of the attorneys you have listed. You may have some of your own, but make sure to ask about these.

Lawyers are highly trained professionals, but they are people too. They have different approaches to life and personalities that they bring with them to the practice of law. It is important that you find someone who listens to you and in whom you can place your trust and confidence. The divorce experience is unpleasant no matter how amicable it is. There is no sense for there to be added tension because of your choice of legal counsel.

To help you decide, you will need to interview several of the attorneys on your list. The divorce process will require you to contact the office regularly, and you want to be sure you like the staff as well as the attorney. If after your talks with each on your list you prefer one lawyer but aren't so sure about the staff in the office, talk it over with the lawyer and see if your concerns can be assuaged by the lawyer. Remember, you are the client, and the lawyer wants to help you.

What you are about to begin is a two-way relationship. The lawyer and you will both need to want to work together for optimum results with the least effort and cost. Now, let's make those calls.

First contact with the lawyer's office

Talking to the office staff. First, find out the location of the office and how easy it will be for you to get to them. This is important, but not the key issue unless transportation is a problem for you. If you have a transportation problem, you will want to find an office that is easy for you to get to whether by public transportation, taxi, or a friend.

You will want to ask the staff if the firm has multiple locations in your town. If they do, be sure to find out whether the attorney you like travels to the other locations or is stationary. Once you know the lawyer you want to meet is in an office location you can get to, your next focus is cost.

Some law offices have flat fees for amicable divorces or a normal hourly fee they will allow their staff to quote to potential clients. Others firms will not allow staff to quote any fees because they want to know your situation and can determine the fee only after they have talked with you.

Either is fine, because every firm will have a quote to provide you for the initial consultation. Sometimes this initial meeting is free, and other times it is a reduced amount, for example, $45 to $100 for a first meeting. Almost all initial consultation fees are limited to one half hour of time. If you meet longer, be prepared to pay the lawyer's normal hourly, just in case. Ask the staff about the firm's fee policy when you schedule the appointment.

Also ask the staff member if there is anything you need to bring to the office or if they have any pre-meeting questionnaire you can complete to facilitate the effectiveness of the meeting. The lawyer's staff may ask you to see the lawyer and find out what is needed or may ask you to bring some of your financial documents to the meeting. This is a matter of preference for the lawyer.

Once you have asked these questions and obtained satisfactory answers, make your appointment with the lawyer. Make sure you see at least two lawyers, preferably three, before you decide. This is very important if you are choosing from a phonebook ad or a television ad, or even if you got the name from a friend or a referral service. Finding the right lawyer is essential to making sure you have the best potential for success. This does not mean you will get everything you want, but you will be more likely to have reasonable expectations for your outcomes. Not everything is up to your lawyer. You and your spouse and his or her lawyer, as well as the judge assigned to the case, are all important players and influence the outcome of the case.

Make a note of how the office staff treated you. Were they courteous? Were they helpful? Did they put you on hold too long? Just make a note of how you felt talking with the lawyer's staff. You may find that once the divorce begins, you will be talking to the staff more than to the lawyer, especially if the issues are settled by agreement. In domestic cases, a client and a lawyer's staff will need to work together well whether the case is settled by agreement or contested.

Once you have called the offices and made your appointments, get ready to meet your lawyer.

9
What Is Your Planned Outcome?

9

What Is Your Planned Outcome?

The first step to getting what you want out of life is this:
Decide what you want.

—BEN STEIN

The meeting with the lawyer. Be prepared. This will allow you to best use both your time and that of your lawyer. It will also save you lawyer's fees. If you are able to consider what you want as an outcome before your meeting, you will be able to ask questions you need answers to, and it will make the meeting much more productive. These tips should help you be prepared and get the most from your half-hour consultation so you can make an informed choice about who you want to hire for this process.

In this section we are focusing on amicable, uncontested divorce, and in the next chapter we will go through a contested process.

Let's get started.

How do I know what I want?

When you reach the decision that divorce is the right choice, then your next step is to decide what you want from the divorce. Think of what will make you the happiest, that is, the best outcome. Is it to get back together with your spouse? Is it to be fair so you can be friends with your spouse when all is over? Is it to punish your spouse for whatever reason you may have? What is your desired outcome? This will affect the lawyer's approach in helping you reach your goal. Is your choice to be amicable because your desires are consistent with your spouse's ideas of divorce? This will be a major factor in determining whether your divorce can be amicable.

You should talk with your lawyer in your first meeting about whether you have been able to talk to your spouse before your initial meeting. If the list of items you want has been agreed upon by your spouse, let your lawyers know. Sometimes clients think they know how their spouse will respond to the prospect of divorce even when they haven't discussed it with them. Sometimes clients are right and sometimes they are not. Below are two common situations lawyers face with clients and their spouses.

Client meets with lawyer and says, "My spouse and I are in total agreement, this is what we want." Lawyer drafts a settlement agreement using the terms provided by the client. Client must now have spouse sign the agreement. The client and spouse argue until midnight over the terms and finally go to bed. The other spouse says, "If you don't make that change we argued over, I'm getting my own lawyer, and I will fight you over that." Now you have to let the lawyer know his or her plan because this was not your expected outcome. You also need to be prepared for additional fees, probably hourly fees, until the divorce is decided by a judge or the issue is resolved between you and your spouse.

Here is another common example. Client meets with lawyer and says, "Spouse doesn't want this divorce. We haven't talked because I am afraid of what will happen. Spouse has a bad temper and in the past has said, 'If I leave it will be the last thing I do.' I am afraid of how spouse will react, but please draft the settlement agreement for us on these terms." Client takes finished agreement to spouse who instead of coming unglued as expected, calmly reads and signs the agreement.

Clients don't always know how their spouses will react to settlement documents, but it is important for you, the client, to have given this some thought. Most of the time, you will know how your spouse will react, and most of the time, they will do exactly as expected. Your opinion is important in helping your lawyer know how to guide you.

It is important for you to know that this first planned

outcome may change. You may change your mind after talking to your lawyer, and as things progress, you may change your mind yet another time. But when you go to your lawyer's office, you should have a clear plan in mind of what you want the outcome to be.

Lawyers who specialize in family law are used to seeing clients in various states of distress. They have generally chosen the field of family law because they understand what it takes to get a successful result for their client. They will know the family court judges and the processes and laws where they practice, enabling them to provide insight into your particular situation. The lawyer you decide to work with should be able to give you a good idea of whether your desired outcome is realistic. Sometimes, clients come in having no idea what they want, making the already difficult process of divorce more costly and emotionally volatile. Some clients want the sun, the moon, and the stars and the lawyer's job is to bring them down to earth. Some clients want to give away everything and walk away with nothing, and the lawyer's job is to bring this decision into perspective as well.

Do I have to change my name?

This decision needs to be made up front. You can change your mind if you asked for a name change in the petition, but you can't add it in later if you didn't request it, at least not without additional expense. You and your spouse can include the name change in any agreed-upon settlement as well. Talk to your lawyer about the issues surrounding a name change so you can determine what you want to do.

How long will a divorce take?

The next question the client asks is almost always about the length of time to conclude the process. The surer you are of what you and your spouse want, the more likely you will have a speedy—and less costly—divorce. This is something you should have a good understanding of when you go to your lawyer's office for the first time.

It is best if you and your spouse can agree upon the outcome and develop the outcome together, but if that is not possible, you should make an effort to find things to agree upon in order to reduce the cost, both emotionally and financially, that accompanies arguments. The more clarity you provide the lawyer at the start, the easier it will be for you get your desired outcome for the least cost. Being wishy-washy and changing your mind on issues creates a lot more work for the lawyer, who in turn will charge you more money. The lack of clear communication will also cause you a lot of additional time as well.

Ask your lawyer what is a typical timeline for divorce when it is settled by agreement and when it is not. Your lawyer should be able to give you a good description of the general process and the costs and time for getting to the end. Every state has its own rules and procedures which must be complied with for a divorce to complete. Some states have laws that prohibit remarriage within a certain amount of time, and others have laws regarding your behavior with your spouse during the divorce. Reconciliation in some states requires a stop of the divorce process and in others it does not. Make sure your lawyer explains anything you want to know, and make sure you completely understand what you are told. Communication is a major issue here. This is your divorce and the lawyer is there to guide you, counsel you, and take you through the process with the least amount of pain from the legal side of the system.

The win-win solution: mediation

Sometimes the parties can put the lawyer on hold while they attempt to work out the issue between themselves. Sometimes the lawyer may recommend mediation for the disputed items so the couples can remain in control of the outcome of the divorce. Mediation is a required process in some states. Find out what is required in your state and be aware that even when forced, the parties are sometimes able to resolve very prickly issues because of the mediator's facilitation. The mediation process is often extremely useful in resolving disputes so a contested divorce can return to one that is agreed to amicably. Keep this in mind even if you are later in a contested divorce. Mediation can be a way to restore sanity to your emotions and finances and obtain a reasonably satisfactory outcome. Most parties who engage in mediation are not totally satisfied with the outcome because they must compromise, a key component of mediation. The advantage to mediation over the court process is you decide how to resolve an issue and how much you will compromise with your spouse versus a court making the decision on your behalf.

I don't want this divorce. Help!

Court-enforced marriage counseling. Because there is a societal preference for marriages to remain intact, some states have a procedure for forcing couples into counseling. It may seem strange, but it can be a success. Much depends on the choice of counselor. Talk to your lawyer and find out whether there is a process for court-ordered counseling in your state and whether the counselor can be proposed by the parties or is chosen by the court or through some other process. Sometimes the court will ask both sides to agree from a list provided by the court, and sometimes the parties can make their own list of counselors and pick someone by mutual agreement. Even when a counselor is not chosen by the parties, there is an added degree of seriousness when counseling is court ordered. Parties are required to attend, and failure to do so without good cause or in some cases permission of the court can result in civil penalties and fines or even sanctions in the proceedings. If a party is absent, the court decides to take an action that is generally harmful to the case of the offending party, for example, a party may be held in contempt of court. This may even carry jail time.

These kinds of powers being held over someone's head can have the effect of a child who has been forced by a parent to sit down, and although he inwardly says, "I may be sitting down, but inside I'm standing up," this inward rebellion doesn't matter because the result is that the child is sitting down. Court-ordered counseling works in much the same way. A spouse has refused all efforts you have made to save the marriage through counseling which the court now orders. The result is the spouse will have to attend counseling.

If your desire is to save your marriage, a motion for court-ordered counseling is clearly worth your time and money. Even in states where there is no statutory authority for court-ordered counseling, a well-written motion may obtain a stay (a hold on the process) of the divorce proceedings for ninety days while you seek or attempt to seek counseling. In some states, this may be the only delay you get, but if you can get your spouse to go to the counseling during that time period, it may well be worth the effort. Divorce is often a wake-up call for the spouse who doesn't want the divorce to appreciate the seriousness of what their spouse has been saying to them, either out loud or by their actions. It is extremely uncommon for one spouse to be oblivious to the hurt, discontent, or anger of a spouse who is unhappy in a relationship.

If you are seeing signs of your spouse's unhappiness, do something about it. Open the lines of communication. Make an effort to be joyful yourself. Try to do something to please your spouse and let them know you intend to work through the problems with them. The key is starting the dialogue. If you don't know why your spouse is unhappy and don't investigate, you can't do anything to improve things. You may find out things you don't want to hear but need to hear. It is extremely rare that relationships die from the action or inaction of only one spouse—almost one-hundred percent of the time, both parties have a part to play in the decline of the relationship. Sometimes all it takes is for real effort to be put into the relationship to revive the spark for the unhappy spouse, who can then choose to withdraw or stay the court proceedings, while the two of you work to restore your marriage.

Keep in mind that if you are serious about saving your marriage, even if the divorce proceeding has begun, don't give up. Many times parties can restore the broken relationship once they realize how deeply their spouse feels about them.

10
To Fight or Not
To Fight,
That Is the Question

10
To Fight or Not To Fight, That Is the Question

He who knows when he can fight and when he cannot, will be victorious.

—SUN TZU

You and your spouse have talked. It is clear you don't agree on much. What do you do now? This is a very common situation when it comes to divorce. Every lawyer hopes her client will reconcile because that is normally the best outcome for all, but it is not always possible. This is when your choice of lawyer becomes critical.

Your lawyer: counting the cost in money and time

She cried, and the judge wiped her tears with my checkbook.

—TOMMY MANVILLE, (MARRIED 13 TIMES, TO 11 WOMEN)

You will want to know if the lawyer has handled other contested divorces. If so, you will want to ask how many and what issues were involved. Were the issues similar to yours? What kinds of results were obtained for the client with your desired outcomes? Find out whether the lawyer has ever appealed any divorce court rulings. The most important thing is not that your lawyer did it, but that the issues were taken up by either someone in his or her firm or someone associated with your lawyer. It will be important to know how many in that context have been appealed, what issues were involved, and how successful it was for the client. Appeal of any ruling by a court is expensive, and in most states there is generally a significant amount of discretion given to the family court judges, so taking an appeal is unusual. Successful appeals on any issue show that the lawyer you are considering is competent and knows the law. If they have not handled the appeals themselves, then it shows that your lawyer appreciates his level of expertise and associates with similar competent lawyers when he or she needs to do so to benefit the client. On the other hand, if the lawyer has handled a significant number of unsuccessful appeals, it is important to understand what went wrong. Too many appeals without any success may indicate the lawyer is just doing it to appease a client even when success is not probable.

It will be important for you have a clear understanding of the general cost of a contested divorce (a range should be available) as well as a general time frame to conclude it. The lawyer should be able to give you an hourly fee charge and an approximation of the time involved depending on certain aspects of the process. For instance, will you need a temporary restraining order or an order for temporary support or use of the house, or custody of the children? If so, the costs will go up.

Can I pay my lawyer on a contingency fee basis?

Contingency fees are a very popular method of getting a lawyer to work a case when you are injured. They allow the lawyer to be paid from the proceeds of the award you receive. The client is usually required to pay only the costs, oftentimes advanced by the lawyer. Contingency fees in divorce proceedings are typically disallowed in most states. Often the law prevents the lawyer from advancing costs to the client as well. This requires the client or the spouse to be able to pay the lawyer.

Can someone other than me pay my lawyer?

If a third party pays the attorney fees, it is critical to make sure the lawyer signs a conflict waiver with you and the third party. This document will clearly spell out the process of who is in control of the litigation and that you are designated the client, not the third party, and only you are provided the privileged information.

Sometimes when a family member is paying the bills, they want to know what they are paying for and it becomes difficult if they want you to approach the divorce one way and you want to do another. Because they are paying the bill, the third party can feel entitled to have a say. It is important that this be addressed up front with the third party and lawyer and yourself before the lawyer is retained. The third party should generally not be allowed in the consultation room because they are not covered by the client privilege, unless there is a valid need for them to know what is being said. This can occur when a third party is also going to be a witness for you.

Can I use my house to pay my lawyer?

You and your lawyer should discuss this approach because there are risks involved. Depending on whether you obtain a loan or actually use a deed, different issues arise because this is an asset that most couples own jointly. That usually means one spouse needs the permission of the other to take a loan against the property or sell it. (See the chapter on Dividing the Pie for more on assets in a divorce proceeding.)

What are the fixed costs?

Because divorce is so fact-based and personality-based, there is no way a lawyer can tell you exactly what your specific contested divorce will cost. However, there are court costs such as filing fees and service of process costs that are set by the state or county where you file, and your lawyer should be able to give you this set-cost information. Also, the lawyer may be able to provide an estimated range for what certain procedures like temporary support orders may cost. If your matter is contested, there will be the need for a court reporter to transcribe the depositions and for any necessary hearings. This means you will be paying for the reporter's time and for the transcripts of the deposition. Depositions are usually taken of witnesses and almost always of you and your spouse if a matter is contested.

Interrogatories, a set of questions for your spouse to answer, will also be sent to limit the issues and to make sure both parties have information about the issues before the proceeding begins. Interrogatories don't usually have a cost other than the time to respond to them. Frequently, they will be accompanied by request for documents. Collecting the necessary documents can be time consuming.

Many states now have an early case conference where each party gives the documents they intend to rely upon in the divorce to the other side. This is done in an effort to save the parties costs and fees. Your lawyer will know what is done in your jurisdiction. But make sure you discuss this together so you understand your responsibility to provide all the documents necessary. Hiding a document or intentionally trying to leave out something important can be a serious problem later in the case. Talk to your lawyer about what your responsibility is so you are ready to partner with him for a successful outcome.

Witness fees. Depending on the issues, in some cases you will need to have expert witnesses testify on your behalf. In most states, a witness fee must be paid to a testifying witness, and there are also costs for issuing a subpoena and having it served on the witness. This is true even for the friend you bring to establish you are a resident of the county and state where the proceeding is held. Some states allow for residency to be established by notarized affidavit, in which case your witness does not appear in court and instead supplies the court required testimony in their affidavit, which is filed with the court. Again, this is something you should talk about with your lawyer.

Getting someone to appear in court for you. Subpoenas are served by process servers and are used to ensure court attendance of the witness. When no subpoena is issued and the witness does not appear, the judge may force the proceeding to continue without your witness. In some situations, judges can issue bench warrants to pick up a witness who does not appear but was subpoenaed. This can sometimes make or break your case. Talk this over carefully with your lawyer and make sure you know the potential risk of your decision to issue subpoenas.

Expert fees and costs for their appearance in court may not be known because in the beginning you may not know all the issues to be decided by the judge and therefore may not know what experts or witnesses you will need. The actual costs you incur will always be dependent on the type of witness needed to present your case, how many you need, and what they must do for you.

If an expert witness writes a report, you will pay a fee. Sometimes these costs can be paid to the lawyer in installments, but generally, the expert will want to be paid for the work performed and court attendance prior to testifying. Your lawyer will know the cost charged by the experts and the other parts of the process so you can make a better financial plan for paying the legal fees and costs.

Motions for support and other things. It is sometimes possible for the lawyer to get his fees from your spouse, but unless your spouse agrees with you to pay the costs and fees, temporary attorney fees must be ordered by the court. Whether a temporary order for legal fees is possible in your situation is another item you should discuss with your lawyer.

The more special orders and hearings needed, the more the cost of your divorce will be. Things like domestic violence or temporary restraining orders may be set up in your state as a do-it-yourself process. You should discuss this with your lawyer. In some states the domestic violence order or temporary restraining order may also provide for use of the home and temporary custody and support. Talk about these things with your lawyer and make sure you know what your options are.

What if I have no money?

If you are without resources—what the court calls indigent—there are special forms you can file to allow the clerk of court to waive certain court fees for you. If you don't have an attorney to ask, check with your local law librarian, clerk of court, sheriff or police department, or even some women's shelters to find out what the procedure is where you live. Some states have a legal-aid service that can assist you and provide you with a lawyer. If you are in a situation in which you have no money or resources, you may also be able to set up a half-hour free consultation with a lawyer. If you live in an area with a law school, check to see whether they have legal assistance available to you. These programs are a good resource for low-cost or no-cost legal advice. In some states, third-year law students who are part of a university program may be allowed to represent you in court. You may even find a law professor who will take your case pro bono without fees to you. You may also find a family lawyer who will work with you on a pro bono basis. Lawyers often do pro bono work as part of their state license requirements. Only the lawyer can decide whether he or she is willing to assist you at no cost, but if you don't ask, you won't know what they will say.

Additional costs of the process. In addition to the motions for temporary support or other preliminary orders, depositions, interrogatories, and other potential costs, if you are in a fight for custody, there are some additional things to talk to your lawyer about. Will a home study or investigation be required? If so, who will perform it and what, if anything, will it cost? How will the investigator be chosen? What about psychological evaluations of the family members—can or will they be required? What is the process and how much will it cost? Is there a state proceeding such as a court-ordered process to have someone evaluated because they threaten to harm themselves or others? Will there need to be depositions taken? What will they cost, and how many will be needed? Will mediation be available or is it required? How much will it cost?

If you have debt, houses, boats, cars, other assets to be divided, children, or pets, divorces get a lot more complicated. If you and your spouse can decide on how to divide the assets and liabilities, visitation, custody, and support, the process will go more smoothly. Perhaps it can even be uncontested. If these decisions cannot be reached by you and your spouse, talk to your lawyer about them to see what is recommended. It is possible that no matter how much you want a certain outcome, the lawyer may know that the law in your state will not allow that result, or that it is not going to happen without agreement from your spouse.

What outcome you are seeking is just as important when the divorce is contested as when it is not. You want to be sure you are able to take care of yourself. If you have children, you will need to think about who is to get custody. What kind of support will be needed? What kind of visitation? Is there a lot of debt or none? Do you and your spouse both work? Are either of you stay-at-home parents? Do you have pets? These are things you should try to decide what the best outcome will be before you see your lawyer. You will find a chapter on each of these issues for a more detailed look.

Contested divorces are tough on everyone in the process, including the lawyer. You need an experienced, knowledgeable lawyer advocating for you in this emotionally charged and highly regulated arena, and you must be confident he will fight hard for you while helping you be realistic with your desired outcomes.

11
Dividing the Pie

11
Dividing the Pie

A sheep might be still while getting shorn, but not when he's getting butchered.

—FRED THOMPSON, FORMER U.S. SENATOR

In order for the judge or your lawyer to advise you about what is and is not possible in the areas of support, property, and debt, there must be a clear appreciation of the family's income, lifestyle, and debt. It is for this reason you will need to know what is going on financially in your household. This will be more difficult if you don't handle the finances, but it must be done.

Let's talk assets

A man in his home is like a piece of Kleenex. He should be ready to be thrown out at a moment's notice.

—RON SHELLEY, CRIMINAL LAWYER

Spouse talk. If possible, you and your spouse should discuss the entire financial picture together so that you will both have a clear understanding. The court and each of your lawyers will need to know about your financial state. Because this area is a major reason couples break up, it may also help you understand why you are in a divorce proceeding or are thinking about one.

Here is a partial list of marital assets you and your spouse should talk about (if you are talking to each other) in order to determine whether your divorce is one of agreement.

1. Income

- Are both of you working? If not, who is at home?
- If so, how much do you each earn? Do either of you earn commissions tips or bonuses? How much?
- Is anyone self-employed?
- Do you own a business?
- What assets do you have individually? Where did they come from? How are they held? (Are they in a joint or single-name bank account or under the bed mattress?)

- What are your plans for emergency funds?
- How will the day-to-day finances be handled?
- What financial accounts do you have—checking accounts, savings, money markets? What amount is in each, where are they located, and what are the account numbers?
- What kind of life insurance do you have? Is it whole, universal, or term-life? Does it have accumulated value, and if so, how much? Who owns the policy and who is beneficiary? What company is the life insurance with and what is the policy value?
- What other insurance do you have, such as mortgage, car, disability, cancer, or long-term care?
- Do you have certificates of deposits or other financial accounts such as brokerage accounts, 401(k)s, or other similar retirement accounts? If so, what are the account numbers and amounts in them, and where are they held? Do you get the stock certificate or is it held by the broker?
- Where are the important papers kept?
- Do you have current wills? (These should be changed following the divorce, so talk to your lawyer about it.)
- Are each of you aware of all the finances of the family?

2. *Real and personal property*

- How much real estate do you own? Where is it located? How is it titled? What is its current market value?

- How many cars, boats, planes, trains, trucks, motorcycles, or other vehicles do you own? What is each worth? What make, model, and year are they?
- Do you have any collections? What about your spouse? What kind and what are they worth?
- Do you or your spouse have any antiques, jewelry, furs, grandfather clocks, or other expensive items that have intrinsic value? If so, what are the items? Take photos and describe them. If you need to get appraisals, you can check with your attorney for reputable sources. For real estate, you need an MAI certification for which there will be a cost. Jewelry and fur can usually be appraised by local jewelers and furriers.

3. *Premarital assets*

Do either of you have assets or inheritance you owned prior to the marriage? Was there a gift to your spouse, or do you still own it? This is a question you will want to be sure you talk to your attorney about. The rules for who owns what are very state specific and are often determined by the title to the property, if there is one, where you acquired the property (which state), or where you were married. Ownership of nonmarital property is often a very contentious issue in divorce. One spouse claims, "It's mine, I got it from my grandfather," and the other says, "Yeah, but you gave it to me." Did either of you receive an inheritance during the marriage? This too is important. It may have been yours originally, but depending on what you did with it and whether your spouse agrees, it may now be characterized as marital property and need to be divided between yourself and your spouse. This may also become a bargaining chip to obtain something else you desire, so this is extremely important to talk about with your attorney.

4. *Personal injury settlements*

There are different treatments by the court on these awards depending upon how they were attained. In a personal injury settlement, some of the proceeds may be for back wages (these would be marital assets), some may be for lost consortium (which may or may not now belong to the person to whom it was awarded). There may be a portion awarded for the injury or pain and suffering of the injured party. These are generally considered personal and not marital awards, but they, too, can change character depending on what happened to them, where they are held, and the title of the account they are in. This area will require close examination by your lawyer.

Hiding assets

It is not uncommon in a divorce because of fear or heightened emotions to find one party has cleaned out all the bank accounts and cut off the credit cards. If this has happened to you, it is imperative you advise your lawyer immediately. Joint accounts are just that, jointly owned.

Either party can clear out the joint accounts without the knowledge or permission of the other spouse. If this happens after the divorce is filed, the court may order the return or place a hold on the funds taken. It will be important to monitor the status of any bank accounts if you or if your spouse may be preparing to file a divorce. There are processes a lawyer may use to assist you in recovering certain marital assets.

Do you suspect a fraudulent conveyance of property has occurred?

This occurs when one party secretly sells, assigns, or gives away a marital asset without the knowledge of the other party in order to hide it and not share it in the property division. There are processes your lawyer can use to help you undo these actions if they violate the law. If you discover a property you thought was in your name but isn't, talk with your attorney.

Bills

The key income earner will normally be responsible to pay the bills, but this is not always the case. Also, even when a spouse has no job, the court may divide the debts or order assets sold to pay some of the debt. Be aware of what is available for getting the bills fairly divided in the state where you live. You lawyer will help you with this.

Liabilities

- How much do you pay each month for living expenses?
- How much do you pay to lenders?
- What is the mortgage and car payment?
- Do you have any student loans? If so, how much do you owe?
- How many credits cards do you have? What is the outstanding balance and monthly payment on each?
- How much are your medical bills and prescription costs? Insurance costs?
- What other loans do you have? Do you owe family or friends? If so, who and how much? Who initiated the loan and why?

Understanding your debts and living expenses is a critical component of a divorce. This may be the first time either you or your spouse has been forced to examine the total financial picture of your family. In most relationships one spouse will handle the bills. Sometimes one spouse will earn and spend the money, and the other manages the household costs. It is not uncommon in some marriages that neither spouse has a good understanding of the whole financial picture. Because finances are the number-one reason for marital discord, it is very important to understand exactly what is going on in this area of your marriage. It is often possible that when the complete financial picture is viewed together, a clearer understanding of how finances have impacted your relationship emerges. It is even possible that financial counseling or bankruptcy may be your solution rather than divorce.

Putting your finances at the mercy of the court

Every court proceeding, whether amicable or not, will generally require both parties to complete a financial affidavit. When the court reviews these affidavits from the husband and wife, it can become very clear as to who is paying the bills. It can be a very eye-opening exercise to you and your spouse as well. You will have to complete one of these forms for your lawyer, so you may as well do it now.

Collecting the supporting documents and listing all the assets can be very time consuming, but it must be done. Your lawyer will probably have his own form for this, but doing it now will save you time later. It might even allow you to realize why your spouse has been screaming about the finances. You may find that what you thought was an incidental expense of $20 a week is actually several hundred dollars a week. Do your best and be honest with yourself, and it will help you and your lawyer.

Collecting the documents that support the financial entries, such as bank statements, deeds, payroll check stubs, utility bills, and other such items, will also help you prepare the exchange of documents required by the court in the divorce proceeding.

Divorce

What are marital assets?

There can be a lot of marital assets, especially if you are involved in a divorce. There are many ways to hold property, and how it is held determines who it belongs to, no matter where it might be moved or whatever else happens to it. There are experts available to help you find lost, stolen, or other missing assets that may have been moved by a spouse. These experts are usually expensive, but they may be needed if you are in this situation. Talk with your lawyer about this process and what can and cannot be done in your particular situation.

The law is very concerned with who owns what property. Therefore, a number of different terms have developed to help determine property ownership. Sometimes, it is possible to think you own something, only to find out you don't.

Most marital property is held in joint name with a right of survivorship to the other owner. This means each party owns one half of the asset and that in the event of the death of either owner, the other party automatically owns the entire property. It generally requires both parties to sign for the sale of this type of asset. After a divorce, the title to this type of property may be changed to tenants in common, where each party can sell, give, or otherwise dispose of their half of the property.

In ten states marital property is community property. (The glossary has the complete listing under Property

Titles.) Community property means each spouse has a one-half ownership in the asset and can sell or give away their own half of the asset, but the other half belongs to the other spouse. Sometimes a spouse has a half-interest ownership whether their name is on the asset or not. A less common but important marital ownership is when property is held as tenants by the entirety. This does not give either spouse a one half interest in any marital asset, but it does give them a one-half interest in the entire asset.

Talk to your lawyer about the titles to your assets and the liabilities. This will be a very important part of the process of fairly distributing the assets and liabilities.

Temporary and permanent alimony

Most states help families during the divorce process by making a provision for judges to issue orders of temporary support. When appropriate, this common process kicks in during the divorce proceeding and usually remains in place until the end of the divorce proceeding. If a spouse is not working, then it is common for the spouse who is working to be ordered to make temporary support payments. If there are children, then the temporary support order may also include who lives in the marital home, which is generally assigned to the spouse with custody of the children. Although in the 1970s and 1980s most custody of children was awarded to the wife, this is no longer true.

Many women have become the breadwinners and some

make higher incomes than their husbands when both are working. Many husbands have become more engaged in caring for the children and often work from home or are stay-at-home dads. Whether mom or dad is home will generally make no difference. For temporary support and custody, the courts will look at which parent is the most involved with the children and who is at home with them and try as much as possible not to disturb the status quo without a hearing to show why it should. The court will look at the necessary expenses to determine the support for the children or for alimony. This order is usually temporary and will end at the time the divorce becomes final. Some judges will convert a temporary support order in a final decree of divorce, so the terms of one are important. It is also possible that once all the testimony is in and the order is issued, that the issues of support and custody will be changed.

Property division of retirement accounts or alimony payments or both?

Generally, only spouses from long-term marriages of ten or more years will be able to obtain permanent alimony or a portion of a spousal retirement account. In some states the spouse may get both alimony and part of the spouse's pension or retirement account.

Retirement accounts and pensions are typically treated as marital property and are divided between the spouses like property. They will require a special order or provision in the settlement agreement in order to instruct the retirement account provider to make the necessary changes to separate the portions for each spouse to have their own account. Because this is ownership of property, it is a permanent division and is not affected when a spouse receiving it marries another.

A spouse who has been at home and who has no job skills may be able to obtain alimony. Alimony will allow a homemaker spouse to live while adjusting to divorced life. Normally, there is no state process defining alimony the way each state does with child support. What is provided by the court is usually based on the need of the spouse and the payee spouse's ability to pay it. This is based upon the income of the marriage and the two spouses and is subject to change due to circumstances that change. Support or alimony payments are subject to end if a receiving spouse marries again.

Can I get or will I pay rehabilitation alimony?

This type of support is usually provided to a younger spouse who needs help getting training in order to support themselves. It may be awarded to an older spouse for the same reason. Rehabilitation alimony or support is just that: support intended to provide a spouse a needed education to become a part of the workforce. Rehabilitation alimony is provided for a short time (one to five years) depending upon what kind of education is required to return the spouse to the marketplace.

Talk to your lawyer about what is right in your situation.

12
Exposing Your Life to the Court and Your Friends

12
Exposing Your Life to the Court and Your Friends

You already have zero privacy—get over it.

—Scott McNealy

When you make a decision to get a divorce, you make a decision to open some of the most personal, private moments of your life to third parties. If you are a public figure, celebrity, or other locally known individual, or if your spouse fits in one of these categories, get ready to have your divorce opened to the world even more than normal. Just as with Prince Charles and Lady Diana, Tiger Woods, and Sandra Bullock, your life can become the nightmare from which you hope for a speedy wake-up call. Even when you are not a celebrity, all of the papers you file in the divorce are generally public records unless your lawyer files a special motion with the court to seal them. Some states are reluctant to do this, so check with your lawyer about how you can protect your privacy.

Releasing control of your life to a judge

I was married by a judge. I should have asked for a jury.

—GROUCHO MARX

Divorce proceedings are trials and in many states they are held in courtrooms open to the public because that is the typical rule for trials. Most states now have judges who only hear legal family matters, and many have completely separate courtroom faculties for family proceedings. Generally, if you want the process private, make sure you discuss your desire with your lawyer. Some states allow television cameras in the courtroom, and this public televising may include proceedings.

Closure of the courtroom is not automatic. Some places will hold divorce proceedings in public unless there is a court order to close the courtroom to the public. There are some courts that hold divorce proceedings in judge's chambers as a matter of practice. This does allow for more privacy and no motions are required. Your lawyer can let you know what to expect.

Even if you are able to obtain an order to close the proceedings to the public or the hearing is held in judge's chambers, there is still the necessity to have people who know you testify on your behalf or for your spouse. This can be embarrassing for some people and perhaps for you. It may cost you a friendship depending on whether the friend testifies for or against you.

"Against me?" you say. "How can that be, if they are my friend?" Unfortunately, this is a very common occurrence when divorce proceedings are contested. The reason is that the facts must be established by witnesses. You and your spouse will not be a lot of help. Generally speaking, if one spouse says something is black, the other spouse will say it is white. It is almost impossible for a judge, who does not know either of you, to know who is telling the truth. This means the more unbiased the testimony that can be provided to support your claim of black or the spouse's claim of white, the more likely the judge will accept the testimony as accurate. Your lawyer will talk to you about this in detail so that you understand the importance of good witnesses.

There is also no "friend" privilege. That means that the friend to whom you confided your deepest thoughts is now compelled to tell the court and whoever is present, under oath and on the witness stand, about those secrets. You may have heard about spousal privilege that states one spouse can't be compelled to testify against the other. In divorce, this doesn't count either. The rules of perjury, lying under oath, and admitting to crimes (which can be prosecuted) still exist. Be careful in this area and talk with your lawyer and prepare him or her for anything your spouse might bring up in this area. Examples: One spouse declares under oath she filed a separate tax return because the spouse failed to disclose income on his. One spouse knows about a crime committed by the other (usually has to do with abuse or drugs) and is prepared to testify about it. You may even have a spouse deny they have obtained a settlement award or call a worker's compensation award (joint property) as a personal injury award (personal to the spouse injured). Make sure you are open and honest with your lawyer about everything. Your lawyer can plan for what he knows, but he cannot plan for a surprise. And getting a second chance to talk about it in court may not always be possible. The court has a rule that says if you should have known about it and don't because you didn't do your homework, you won't get a chance later. So don't keep it back from your lawyer. Let him or her decide what needs to be done in the situation by talking it over with you.

Witnesses will generally need to be deposed, which requires a formal process. You, your lawyer, your spouse and his or her lawyer, a court reporter, and the witness will all be in attendance. Even though it is your divorce, the lawyers will often ask questions about the life of the friends who are testifying. This questioning can make them uncomfortable or pry into their personal lives, but it is generally done to show there is a bias or to determine the credibility of the witness.

Unique situations to consider

You will need to talk with an attorney in your area to find out how the law in your state addresses each of the following issues. Each circumstance may bring a different set of problems depending on the other facets of your marriage.

Is either party a dual citizen or an immigrant?

Whether either party holds a dual citizenship may not matter at all, but in certain situations, it may be extremely important. This is particularly true when custody and visitation of children is involved. There are many cases of parental kidnapping by the non-U.S. citizen to their native country. These cases involve international law and can be extremely difficult and costly to pursue.

Citizenship may also come into play in the process of serving the foreign-born spouse. If they are in their home country visiting or living and not in the U.S. at the time the divorce is being initiated, getting them properly served and having the right to bring them to court may be a problem. If the foreign national is a legal immigrant here on a visa or green card, the divorce may impact their right to remain in the United States, and this and other immigration-related issues may need to be addressed along with the divorce.

All of these things need to be examined closely by your attorney to provide you the best advice in your situation.

Is either party on active duty?

If one or both of the marriage partners are in the military and both are currently stationed in the same place, there is usually no issue in obtaining a divorce. If one marriage partner is overseas, then special rules apply under federal law for the protection of the service person who is out of the country. If the marriage has lasted ten years or longer, and the spouse has been in the military ten years or longer, there is federal law that must be taken into account regarding the service person's pension. Your attorney should know these things and be able to discuss your rights under these laws.

Are there medical issues?

Is either party disabled or mentally incapacitated? Is there a medical issue such as a coma? Is either party in a rehabilitation facility or a psychiatric institution? Each of the these situations is similar but may have a different approach based on the law in the state where you live. Almost every state will have a special process for divorce when the spouse being divorced is incapacitated, whether it is for physical, mental, or psychological reasons. Some states allow divorce to proceed but require a certain amount of time to pass between the filing of the divorce and the actual dissolution of the marriage. Others require special hearings on the spouse's capacity. Check with your lawyer to find out what applies in your state.

Is either party in a prison facility of any kind?

When a spouse is in prison, the problems that arise are generally about service of process and obtaining depositions. Spouses who are in prison may complicate resolution of issues such as custody, support, and visitation as well. This is an area where your lawyer needs to be fully informed so you can obtain the advice you need.

Has your spouse abandoned you? Do you know how to get in touch with your spouse, his family, or his friends?

These issues are also related. If you have had no contact with your spouse for a long time, you may believe you have been abandoned. The law in each state will prescribe the length of time that determines abandonment and how you may proceed to divorce the spouse you cannot find. If you do not know how to contact any friends or family of your spouse, it will be important to the divorce for you to attempt to locate them. Contact a best friend, a coworker or boss, even their mom, dad, sister, or cousin. You will need to show the court you have made reasonable efforts to locate your spouse. Your lawyer will know how to proceed and what legal requirements need to be met in order to serve your spouse by publication rather than personal service. Service by publication is extremely technical and if not done correctly, will be ineffective.

Bigamy

This may seem an unusual topic for a book on divorce, but it is something that does come up from time to time. When a spouse discovers they are still married to a former spouse, it can be a real shock. It usually happens when one party thinks they are divorced, but the other party failed to complete the process. It can happen intentionally, but that is less common. It can also occur when you have lived in a state that recognizes common-law marriages, but when the breakup happened, everyone went their separate ways, not realizing they were actually married because they had not participated in a ceremony.

When either partner is married, they have no capacity to get married to anyone else, making any subsequent attempt to marry void. Getting the proper annulment or divorce and remarriage to your current spouse will be something you need to discuss with your lawyer. If you find yourself in this situation, seek immediate legal advice because bigamy is a felony in most states.

Fraudulent identity

This situation occurs when you marry someone who is using an alias so that you believe you are marrying a different person than the one you married. An example of this occurred some years ago when a woman married a man named Joe Montana. She believed him to be the wealthy, well-known professional football player. After the marriage she discovered he was not the Joe Montana she thought he was and wanted an annulment or divorce. Unfortunately, she went through the marriage ceremony and said "I do" to this Joe Montana. He may not have been who she thought he was, but the court left her marriage intact because she knew she was marrying the man who stood with her at the altar even though she thought from his name he was someone else. You marry David Jones only to later find out he is John Lockhart. You have still married the man, not the name.

If you find yourself in this type of situation, see how your state handles it. It may have a different result, and your lawyer can let you know whether annulment or divorce will be available to you.

13
Are There Children?

13
Are There Children?

Parenthood is a lot easier to get into than out of.

—BRUCE LANSKY

Paternity issues and divorce

Is there any question regarding the paternity of any children? If there is, now is the time for the paternity test. If the divorce proceeds and all children born to the wife during the marriage are presumed to be issue (a legal way of saying children) of the marriage, this means the court makes a presumption that any child born to the wife is her husband's child. If you are concerned this may not be the case, this is one of those times where you need to speak up.

If you don't speak up now and your divorce completes, you may find yourself supporting another man's child until he or she is twenty-six (the age when children are no longer entitled to be on their parents' health care coverage).

Your lawyer will talk with you about the blood tests that must be taken by mom, dad, and child to determine whether the DNA is from the marriage. Once a divorce is over, so is your chance of forcing a determination of a child's paternity.

Adopted children

Time and experience have taught me a priceless lesson:
Any child you take for your own becomes your own if you
give of yourself to that child.
I have born two children and had seven others by adoption,
and they are all my children, equally beloved and precious.

—DALE EVANS, ADOPTIVE PARENT

In a divorce, adopted children are treated like any natural child of the marriage, unless they are adopted by a stepparent. For this reason, the information provided about custody, support, and visitation will apply to adopted children of the marriage.

When a boy or girl is the natural child of one of the spouses in the marriage and the other spouse adopts them, the courts sometimes treat the adoption differently. Each state has their own laws about how an adoption can take place, so your lawyer should be told about the adoption and guide you toward the best solution.

Stepchildren are often allowed to continue to inherit from their natural parents. The natural parent has only given up the right to visit or custody of the child. In exchange they are released from their support obligation for the child. If a couple divorces and the stepchildren no longer wish to have a relationship with the stepparent, in some situations this is allowed. Talk to a local lawyer to see how stepparent adoptions work in a divorce where you live.

Custody, visitation, and shared parental rights

In spite of the six thousand manuals on child raising in the bookstores, child raising is still a dark continent and no one really knows anything. You just need a lot of love and luck—and, of course, courage.

—BILL COSBY

Children from birth to age four. The issues surrounding children of the marriage are often determined by the age of the children. If the children are very young, the courts often lean toward providing custody to the parent who is at home with them the most. Under what is known in law as the "tender years" doctrine, very young children are generally allowed to remain with their mother, though this is not a hard and fast rule and is not automatic. A mother who can be shown to be unfit to handle the parental obligation will not be awarded custody of even a newborn. Establishing that either parent is unfit is not easy but can be done if there is a real issue. Many parents, who are great with their children, seem to grow two heads when a divorce begins. Allegations of all sorts fly back and forth as each parent tries to outdo the other for custody. The key is not what you say but what can be proven.

Sometimes, even when child abuse has been proven against a parent, the guilty parent will still have the ability to see the child, usually in a restricted or controlled environment, and will have an obligation to support the child. In other situations where abuse has been proven, a parent's parental rights are completely severed by the court. When this occurs, the custodial parent has what is known as sole custody of the child. The court may or may not require support from the absent parent in this situation. These are very fact-sensitive situations, and the attorney you are working with will be able to advise you according to your own situation.

Children ages ten and up. When your children are older, it is possible that the judge may want to talk to them before deciding on the custodial parent. The information obtained from the children usually helps a judge understand the child's perspective, not to let the children decide where they want to live. The older the children get, the more likely their choice of residence will be granted. Check with your lawyer for how judges decide this in your location.

Split or shared custody

When the parents are struggling with issues of property division, they may still be very committed to their children. When the parents live close enough and the children can attend the same school regardless of the parent with whom they reside, and both are equally able to support the children financially, then the court will sometimes without impact allow what is known as shared custody. The parents must be able to show this is best for the children.

Split custody is when the parents alternate custody or visitation by swapping children on a six-month or annual basis. This type of custody is rarely seen because the courts generally frown on this scheme. If your children are middle-school-aged or older, this may be a solution that works for you, particularly if the children would like to split their time between the parents. But be careful, because what a child thinks about split custody may be useful, but it is not going to be the only concern the court will need to work through before imposing this kind of situation.

Many states have a process known as Shared Parental Rights that allows the noncustodial parent to maintain a say in the activities a child engages in at school or afterward. In theory, this can work well, but in some situations, it can be difficult when parents disagree vehemently about what is best for their child. Your lawyer can help you with these situations also.

Visitation rights

Most courts have a preferred style of visitation they incorporate in their divorce decrees. Many lawyers also have schedules of visitation they prefer to use when there is not one prescribed by the law or the court. Talk with your lawyer about any special issues that you need to address so that you can have a say into how visitation is structured.

For example, most visitation schedules provide the noncustodial parent visitation every other weekend and one day in the middle of the week. If a parent is a shift worker or has a rotating schedule, then a weekend that is normally defined as Friday beginning at 6 p.m. through Sunday at 6 p.m. may not allow the parent to visit his or her child at all. This is clearly something to be addressed either during the negotiation with your spouse or to request from the court after the trial so that your "weekend" is correctly allowed in the decree. This may also be the case if a parent goes from a Monday-to-Friday workweek to a job with shifts or rotations or at night.

Child support

Child support in many states is set by formula. Because of the way the statute is written in some states, judges have little or no discretion in the area of support. They look at the financial affidavits of the parties and apply the formula, and that is what is awarded. This can often be a matter of serious contention when the noncustodial parent must pay support and is not employed or is underemployed. When the parties share physical custody, there may be some adjustments to the state schedule. Because the court wants children to be supported, it may not be adjustable. Check with the lawyer in your state to see how the child support formula is applied. Some states operate from gross pay and others from net pay. Some will allow the parties to make agreements, and others go strictly by the formula. The formula generally includes the income of both parents. Some formulas will consider expenses, but the intent of the process is to even out the dollars.

Different states have come up with their own plans for courts to make support awards. One factor seen often is how much time the child spends with the absent parent. The closer the number reaches six (6) months, the more likely the court is to adjust the state formula.

There are rare instances in which both parents are equally able to provide for the children and have shared or split physical custody as opposed to shared parental rights. In these cases, no support is ordered to be paid by either parent. They instead split evenly all the costs of clothing, food, and shelter and meet any other needs.

Support issues are usually the most highly charged issues of the divorce, which is not difficult to understand because of the financial pressures to the marriage in general. It is common for a noncustodial parent to resent the support paid when visitation is problematic, even though the two are generally not tied together. Because of the noncustodial parent's resentment or control issues, he or she will refuse to pay support, pay it slowly, or try to tie the hands of the receiving spouse when it comes to how the support is to be spent. It is important to know that the use of the support is for the custodial parent to decide. It may be used for household expenses or food or whatever the custodial parents believes is appropriate to meet the needs of the household. The one caution in this area would be this. Don't spend the child support on luxury items if the children are going without food or other necessities. If this happens, the custodial parent may have a problem. The noncustodial parent could argue neglect and seek a change of custody.

ESA: educational saving account

Support of children is the responsibility of both parents. When they live in one home, the costs are generally not identified; they just get paid. If new shoes are needed, they are bought. If school requires money for a child to participate in an activity, it is paid. The child support is intended to assist the custodial parent with those costs and have the noncustodial parent involved in their child's support and upbringing. When it comes to education, the court may require one parent or both to contribute to an educational savings account. They may also merely order one parent to pay for the education in some fashion. The court can order payment with conditions such as the child must go to a state school versus a private school, and the child must perform reasonably well in school. This can be a very important provision in a settlement or a court order of divorce, so be sure to talk about this with your spouse in an uncontested case and with your lawyer if contested.

Medical and dental insurance

Courts may require that insurance is carried by one parent or the other on the children. If the custodial parent has insurance, the court may order the noncustodial parent to pay the premium. This is an area where negotiation may be beneficial to both parties and the children. Talk to your lawyer about the best way to cover this issue. Under the 2010 health care reformation act, medical insurance can be in place until a child is twenty-six years old. Whether you think you will be the custodian of the children is a key area for discussion with your attorney.

Life insurance to protect support obligations

When there are support obligations such as child support or alimony, the court may require an insurance policy on the life of the support-paying spouse to protect the children or the former spouse in the event of death of the support-paying spouse. The policy premium may be paid by either spouse depending on resources. Some spouses would prefer to own and pay the premium to be sure it is in place. Please talk about this issue with your counselor to do what is best in your situation. Sometimes the premium can be characterized as additional alimony or child support. Check with your lawyer on this.

14
What About the Four-Legged Children?

14
What About the Four-Legged Children?

I really love pets. They're like children. They know if you really love them or not. You can't fool them.

—Donna Douglas

The Solomon Solution

Pets are property as are livestock and any other animals you and your family may own. They are personal property and possible marital property depending upon whether they have titles such as thoroughbred horses and dogs and cats. The owners are usually shown on the animal's papers, which may help determine who owns them. The true issue arises when both spouses want to keep the animal.

Many pet owners treat their pets like children. If this is the case, the divorce proceeding may also provide for visitation and custody of the pet like it would for children. If you and your spouse cannot agree, the court will decide, but they may not make the decision you want. They may order the property sold and the proceeds divided between you. They may give custody of the pet to the noncustodial parent of the children, or they may give the pet to the custodial parent because of the children.

The most unusual situation with pets I have encountered was a couple fighting over pet remains in the yard. The spouse who obtained the house argued the remains stayed with the house, while the spouse who wanted them argued they were separate property and was allowed to move the remains to a local pet cemetery where both parties could go. Some judges in family matters are very creative, but the most creative solution is the one you and your spouse can agree upon.

15
Actually Dividing the Household

15
Actually Dividing the Household

She got the gold mine, I got the shaft.

—JERRY REED

Once the decree of dissolution of marriage is final, the next step is to divide the marital assets. When arguments arise over who gets the dishes and who gets the pots and pans, the court will get involved and direct that an inventory and division be made under the watchful eyes of a mutually acceptable third party. Sometimes the party's lawyers will be there. This is never a pleasant process, and most judges don't want to be involved with passing out the forks and knives. From your perspective, it is much better for everyone if you can make the division without involving the court. By this point, nine of out ten times, separations have already taken place and each spouse has what they wanted from the marital home. But there are those situations where it just doesn't happen that way.

If you find that you have been awarded a certain painting or the car and the spouse in possession refuses to release it or give you the title, then you will need to get an order of enforcement from the court. Some states make this a very simple process by allowing you to take your certified copy of your decree to your local sheriff and asking him to help you obtain the property awarded to you. You will need to talk to your attorney to find out the process required in your state.

16
What Happened to the Credit?

16
What Happened to the Credit?

A lot of people have asked me how short I am.
Since my last divorce, I think I'm about $100,000 short.

—MICKEY ROONEY

When financial issues are the main reason given for obtaining a divorce, it may not be a surprise to discover that credit is often another victim of the marriage's demise. When a family is living from paycheck to paycheck after a divorce, it is not uncommon to find that both spouses are now struggling to stay afloat. If the bills and the assets are divided between you and your spouse, and support is being paid by one of you to the other, the same amount of money you had before now has to do more.

There are many ways to repair bad credit if that problem remains now that the divorce is over. If you are the spouse who never handled finances and never had credit in your name, your divorce may have given you bad credit depending on how the bills were handled. You will want to begin to establish credit in your own name and maintain it so that when you need it, it will be there. A good credit counselor or financial planner should be able to help you with this.

Once the divorce is over, many people find themselves needing a second job to try to make up for the loss of income from the division of the marriage. If you obtain a one-time settlement in the divorce, make sure you find someone with good financial expertise to assist you in proper management of the settlement proceeds. Without good money management skills, the settlement may be spent before you realize it. Get the help you need to take care of your credit and your financial security. The resource section contains sources to help you repair your credit.

Credit and changing your name

As discussed in an earlier chapter, a name change can be obtained as part of the divorce. Under normal situations, a name change is a separate legal process with its own requirements and costs. But because you are splitting the couple back into two single persons, it can be done as part of the divorce at no extra charge.

Whether you keep your married name or return to your maiden name is your choice. There are pros and cons for both. When it comes to credit, if you had credit in your maiden name that is still in good condition, it may make sense to return to your maiden name. Today, so much of the credit is tied together that it may make no difference at all. Changing your name will require you to change your identification, social security card, and passport. Mothers often keep the name of their children, but remember, a re-marriage will possibly change the name again.

Talk with your lawyer and make a decision before you end the divorce, because afterward it will be too late. This is one thing that if not addressed during the divorce cannot be done later without an entirely new proceeding.

17
You Want to Go Where?

17

You Want to Go Where?

Life is a quest and love a quarrel.

—EDNA ST. VINCENT MILLAY

Your divorce is finally over. You and your spouse have begun to settle into "life after divorce," and things have begun to look pretty normal. The former spouse has regularly paid their support obligations and exercised their visitation. The children have begun to adjust to their two homes and only seeing the noncustodial parent at certain days and times. Some of the anxiety and fear has begun to subside because of what now looks like the new daily life for everyone.

Then you get a call from the former spouse, or perhaps you make the call to your former spouse. On the other end of the line is this scenario: "Hey, just wanted to let you know I have a new and exciting job opportunity in Somewhere, U.S., and they want me to start in two weeks. I will be taking the kids with me and just wanted to give you a heads-up." This notice is generally required any time one spouse intends to do something that will change the ability of the other spouse to see the children as the visitation agreement provides.

The spouse who receives the call says something like this: "Well that is just great, but the kids will stay with me. I'm not going to lose my right to visit, and if you take them all the way across the country to Somewhere, U.S., I can't see them and won't be able to help rear them."

The response is usually: "I don't care, it's a free country and this is a great opportunity for me and the kids, and I'm going." *Click.*

Is there anything you can do? Maybe, and maybe not. If the decree of divorce does not speak to the issue of what happens when one spouse moves to another part of the U.S. or the world, then you may be able to return to court and get the judge to make a decision. The judge will decide based upon what is in the best interest of the children, not the parents. It is possible for the judge to determine that it is best for the custodial parent to move and take the children and modify the other parent's visitation rights accordingly. It is also possible for the judge to decide to change the parent with custody. This is a more unusual outcome, more likely to occur when children are older and have been in the same school for several years or the same community and are engaged in a number of important activities. But even this will not guarantee that the parent who wants to stop the move can do it.

When there is a change of this nature and the custodial parent will be moving to better their income, or perhaps the move is because your husband or wife's new spouse is being moved with their job, the court may consider a modification of the child support. This is not automatic and must be requested and will depend as before upon the incomes of both parents, but not necessarily on the income of the stepparent if there is one.

If the move is related to the job change of the stepparent, the noncustodial parent may have more ability to prevent the move. These are considerations you and your lawyer will need to discuss as your lawyer will know the law in your area and what the judges in your area are likely to order in your situation. There is no one right answer for everyone. The key here is to know that if you get the phone call from your former spouse, your next phone call should be to your lawyer to find out about your parental rights and how they can be protected.

This is a tough situation if it is not amicably worked out between the parents, but it happens fairly regularly after divorce. The most important thing is to get information about what you can do as soon as possible so you can make the best decision for yourself and your children.

18
It's an Issue of Enforcement

18
It's an Issue of Enforcement

If you think you have trouble supporting a wife,
try not supporting her.

—Anonymous

When a divorce is over, there is often so much animosity between the spouses that they lose sight of the children. When this happens, the noncustodial parent will often decide not to pay the support that has been ordered by the court. If this occurs, an enforcement of the decree of divorce is the next step. Keep in mind that if you and your former spouse can agree upon the terms, they can be put into effect without a court hearing. The exception to this rule is the state enforcement proceeding. Even in the

state process, there is room for the former spouse to nego-
tiate a settlement with the state.

Enforcing child support orders

Most states have a process in which a custodial parent
can get the enforcement done by the district attorney or
state prosecutor's office. Or there may be a contract attorney who has been hired by the state to handle enforcement
proceedings. Check with your lawyer or the local court-
house to see what the arrangement is where you live. When
you use the state process for enforcement, there is generally a lengthy process between your request and seeing any
funds in your account. This is particularly true if you and
your former spouse now live in different parts of the country. If this is the case, there is a federal law that allows your
state to go to the other state for the enforcement process,
and the money is paid to the state where the noncustodial
parent resides and then is sent to you. Most states will de-
duct the cost of any welfare or other social network benefits
that the custodial parent has received from the state due to
the failure to receive child support. Most states will require
the parent seeking welfare or other state benefits to obtain
an order of enforcement for child support in order to get
the food stamps or other state assistance.

When a noncustodial parent is under an enforcement
order and fails to pay support for any reason, the court can

hold that parent in contempt of court and put them in jail to be released upon the payment of the support due the other parent. The Internal Revenue Service will also confiscate any refund due the noncustodial parent and send it to the state to apply to the child support arrearages. It will then be forwarded to the custodial parent. These rules apply regardless of how many marriages or children a noncustodial parent has. The intent of the court is for parents to provide for their own children.

There is also usually a state process for enforcement using private attorneys when the custodial parent is able to pay the fees for a lawyer to assist. In this case, your lawyer should know whether you have begun a proceeding with the state. They will have a number of other questions for you about visitation and support, and you will need to be able to prove what has been paid and how far behind the payments are. Your lawyer can help you decide which approach is best for you to pursue and how likely you are to be successful in your situation.

Enforcing property provisions of divorce decrees

Any part of the decree can be taken to the court for enforcement. If your state doesn't provide a sheriff- or police-assisted process of obtaining your personal property awarded under the decree, your lawyer can file a proceeding with the court to help you get what has been awarded to you. This may be your one-half of the sale of marital property when the other spouse doesn't want to buy you out or sell. The court can assist you in obtaining your personal effects, and if the possessing spouse has sold, destroyed, or given them away, the court can make a provision for restitution to make you whole.

Enforcing visitation rights

If your custodial spouse is preventing you from seeing or talking with your children, or speaks ill of you to turn the children against you, your lawyer may be able to help. You may be able to get a judge to enforce the decree's provision for visitation, and in extreme cases, the court may actually make you the custodial parent. This happens when the court believes you will be more likely to allow your spouse to visit with the children in accordance with the decree's provisions.

Whatever is going on between you and your former spouse that concerns the children may also concern the court. Remember, once you gave your life to the court by going through a divorce, the court will be there until the obligations under the order cease. For child support and visitation, this generally occurs when the children are emancipated or turn eighteen. Check for the law in your state. Sometimes it will not occur until children are out of school, but sometimes it can be sooner if the child marries or enters the military service.

Enforcing alimony

There is generally no state mechanism to enforce payments of alimony in the same manner as child support, but you should check with your state just in case. This is particularly true if you are receiving any kind of state assistance. Otherwise, you will need to talk with your lawyer about enforcing the alimony payments. Fees under the enforcement process may be a percentage of the recovery. The proceeding is another court process, and you must be able to prove what has or has not been paid to the court's satisfaction. If your former spouse is not making the required payments for any reason, contact your lawyer immediately so the proper process can begin as soon as possible.

19
Getting More Than
You Got

19
Getting More Than You Got

Life is just one damned thing after another.

—Elbert Hubbard

Modifying the divorce decree

The general rule to raise or lower child support or alimony, change custodial parents, or convert rehabilitative alimony to permanent alimony is what is called a showing of changed circumstances. This means the person trying to obtain a change must be able to show the court they are in a different situation or that their former spouse is in a different situation from what existed when the decree of divorce was issued.

Depending on what you desire to change and what the facts of the situation are, you may get a modification to the decree. Like the original divorce, if you and your former spouse are in agreement to the change, the agreement can be signed by both of you and filed with the court to modify the original decree and effectuate the agreed-upon change.

It is also possible to return to court and have the judge decide whether to modify the terms of the divorce. This may happen when your former spouse is now making more money, and you want to increase the child support or alimony paid to you accordingly as the cost of living increases. (If there is a settlement agreement, it should include a provision for cost-of-living or inflation adjustments so you don't have to return to court for this type of modification.)

Modification may be requested when the former spouse has less income and wants to reduce payments as any form of alimony or child support. If alimony is modifiable, either party can request a change. In some situations, a spouse who received rehabilitation alimony may be able to convert it to permanent alimony by proving that changed circumstances require it, such as an illness that prevents the spouse from working, or some other unexpected event that prevents the goal of being self-supporting.

Talk with your lawyer about any change in your life or that of your former spouse that you believe may allow you to modify the decree to increase the support you receive or reduce the support you pay. Your lawyer should be able to give you the best advice according to your situation and let you know the cost of trying to get the decree modified, and what the potential outcome is likely to be. Remember, just because you ask doesn't mean you will get what you want, but if you don't ask, there is not a chance you will get what you want. Try to work your issues out with your former spouse first, and then as a last resort, let the court do it for you.

Glossary

Affidavit – a written document stating under oath that the statements made are true and must be signed in front of someone authorized to take oaths, such as a notary public or a county clerk.

Answer – a written pleading that responds to a complaint issued in a lawsuit upon the defendant or respondent where the respondent gives a brief response admitting, denying, or admitting and denying in part to each question asked on the complaint.

Appeal – asking a higher court to review the decision made by a lower court in an attempt to change the decision based solely on the information from the original trial or decision. Time restrictions between the original decision and appeal should be considered by consulting an attorney or court.

Child Support – monies ordered by a court during a divorce or dissolution of marriage, to be paid by a non-custodial parent to a custodial parent for the benefit of a minor; may also include insurance, tuitions, or other expenses incurred on behalf of a minor until at least the child's eighteenth birthday.

Civil Penalties – fines set forth by a government agency for offenses such as paying taxes late or not obtaining a permit.

Community Property – see Property Titles.

Complaint – the first pleading filed with the court to claim someone's legal rights against someone else stating the factual and legal basis for the claim.

Contempt of Court – a judge can hold someone in contempt of court if the person is being rude, disrespectful to an attorney or the judge, or causing any type of disturbance in the courtroom and continues to do so even after being warned.

Contingency Fee Agreement – a written agreement between an attorney and his client that states that the attorney will collect fees only if the matter is won or settled in favor of the client.

Court Reporter – someone who creates a transcript of court hearings, depositions, and other official proceedings.

Custody – typically refers to the court's decision stating which parent will have legal physical control of a minor.

Deponent – refers to the person who is testifying or being questioned during a deposition.

Deposition – the pretrial questioning of a witness under oath in the presence of both sides' attorneys and a court reporter outside of the courtroom.

Domestic Violence – the crime of physically beating a partner, spouse, or parent.

Enforcement Proceeding – a court proceeding held before a judge to enforce court orders.

Expert Witness – witness who is proven to be a specialist in a certain area and offers his or her expert opinion without having actually witnessed the occurrence being questioned.

Forced Rehabilitation – when someone is thought to be a danger to themselves or others, they may be held for seventy-two hours for a mental health evaluation. This can be voluntary or involuntary. Voluntary commitment is when someone, at least eighteen years of age or older, or a guardian of someone under age eighteen applies for mental health evaluation or treatment. Involuntary commitment is when someone is not able to determine that he is a danger to himself or others.

Fraudulent Conveyance – see Property Titles.

Good Cause – legal jargon meaning that the court has sufficient legal reason to make a ruling.

Hearing – a pretrial proceeding held before a judge without the presence of a jury to determine an issue of fact or of law or both.

Indigent – someone who can not afford to hire an attorney.

Interrogatories – series of written pretrial questions asked by the opposing party of a lawsuit to be answered by a set time of receipt under oath.

Joint Property – see Property Titles.

Joint Property with Right of Survivorship – see Property Titles.

Judge – the official authority presiding over court proceedings.

Life Estate – see Property Titles.

Litigant – anyone involved in a lawsuit, including the plaintiff, defendant, petitioner, and respondent.

Loss of Consortium – damage claim used in a lawsuit meaning a spouse cannot have normal marital relations due to injury or mental duress caused by another's actions.

Mediation – an attempt to settle a legal dispute through a third party appointed by the court.

Motion – a written request submitted to the court that a decision be made.

Orders for Counseling – order given by the court for a party or parties to receive outpatient counseling from a licensed mental health professional.

Petition – written request submitted to the court for such things as continuances, modifications to previous orders, reduction of bail, and dismissal of a case.

Pleading – any legal document to be filed with the court is considered a pleading, such as complaints, interrogatories, motions, and petitions.

Proceeding – a court filing, hearing, trial, or judgment in a lawsuit or criminal prosecution.

Property held by Entirety – see Property Titles.

Remainder – see Property Titles.

Request for Documents – the asking of one party to the opposing to examine or copy any documents relevant to a lawsuit.

Residency Witness – someone who testifies to another's residency status in court.

Respondent – the party who responds to a petition.

Restitution – giving property back to the owner or paying for the loss of property.

Restraining Order – an order passed by the court to keep things as they are, such as custody of a child or possession of marital property.

Retainer – advanced payment by a client to an attorney for services to be performed.

Sanctions – penalty imposed by the court upon either an attorney or one of the parties for violating a rule of court or some other penalty issued by the court, or to compensate the other party.

Service of Process – the process of serving papers, subpoena, summons, complaints, et cetera upon a party of a legal proceeding.

Spousal Support – monies ordered by the court to be paid to one ex-spouse by the other during a divorce or dissolution of marriage.

Stay of Proceedings (also Stay) – the ruling of the court to halt further legal proceedings in a trial.

Temporary Orders – temporary ruling by the court until the conclusion of a trial or hearing.

Tenants by the Entireties – see Property Titles.

Tenants in Common – see Property Titles.

Transcript – a written account of legal proceedings such as a hearing, deposition, and testimony.

Trial – the examination of issues of law or fact by disputing parties to be determined by a judge or jury.

Visitation – the time set forth by the court that a noncustodial parent should be able to spend with the minor.

Witness – person who testifies under oath during a hearing, deposition, or trial. May also be someone who signs a document stating they observed an incident.

Property Titles

Community Property – the equal contribution by both husband and wife, even if one contributes more financially to the marriage and during divorce proceedings the property is divided equally despite which party is at fault. Alaska, Arizona, California, Idaho, Louisiana, Nevada, New Mexico, Texas, Washington, Wisconsin, and Puerto Rico recognize community property.

Fraudulent Conveyance – the transfer of property in an attempt to hide it or keep it from creditors.

Joint Tenancy – property owned by both parties that cannot be transferred by one party without the other party's consent; however, if being pursued by a creditor, both parties are held liable.

Joint Tenancy with Right of Survivorship – property that is equally owned by both parties and upon the death of one, ownership transfers fully to the surviving owner.

Life Estate – ownership of property usually decreed by a will and gives survivor the right to occupy the property for the duration of their lifetime.

Remainder – the transfer of real property to someone in a will at the end of another's ownership. For example, John leaves house to Bill for life and leaves house to Bill's son

Junior after Bill's death. Junior has the "remainder."

Tenancy by the Entirety – when property is owned by both parties equally; however, gives each party the right to ownership in full upon the death of the other party.

Tenancy in Common – title of ownership giving each party equal use of property; however, property does not pass immediately to the second party upon the death of the first, and each owner can sell his or her piece without permission of the other owner.

Helpful Reads

Following is a list of best-sellers regarding the topics discussed throughout *Divorce: An Essential Guide to the Inevitable Questions.* In addition to printed sources, one of the best Internet sites for obtaining legal information is Law.com. It can be useful to find cases and other information that may help you.

Abuse/Codependency

Beattie, Melody. *Codependent No More: How to Stop Controlling Others and Start Caring for Yourself.* Center City, MN: Hazelden, 1987. Print.

Evans, Patricia. *The Verbally Abusive Relationship: How to Recognize It and How to Respond.* Holbrook, Mass.: Adams Media Corporation, 1996. Print.

Alcoholism/Addiction

Peck, M. Scott. *People of the Lie: the Hope for Healing Human Evil.* New York: Simon and Schuster, 1998. Print.

Sims, Kecia C. *Loving the Addict, Hating the Addiction: for Christian Families Coping with Drug Addiction.* Lincoln, NE: iUniverse, 2003. Print.

Bankruptcy and Divorce

Elias, Stephen, Albin Renauer and Robin Leonard. *How to File for Chapter 7 Bankruptcy.* Berkeley, Calif.: Nolo, 2009. Print.

Jowell, Barbara Tom., and Donnette Schwisow. *After He's Gone: a Guide for Widowed and Divorced Women.* New York: Citadel, 2001. Print.

Children and Divorce

Dobson, James C. *Bringing Up Boys.* Wheaton, Ill.: Tyndale House, 2005. Print.

Dobson, James C. *Bringing Up Girls: Practical Advice and Encouragement for Those Shaping the Next Generation of Women.* Carol Stream, Ill.: Tyndale House, 2010. Print.

Ricci, Isolina. *Mom's House, Dad's House: a Complete Guide for Parents Who Are Separated, Divorced, or Remarried.* New York: Fireside, 1997. Print.

Credit Repair

Bryan, Mark A., and Julia Cameron. *Money Drunk/ Money Sober: 90 Days to Financial Freedom.* New York: Ballantine Wellspring, 1999. Print.

Kelly, Tom. *The New Reverse Mortgage Formula: How to Convert Home Equity into Tax-free Income.* Hoboken, N.J.: Wiley, 2005. Print.

Leonard, Robin, and John Lamb. *Credit Repair.* Berkeley, CA: Nolo, 2009. Print.

Life after Divorce

Frisbie, David, and Lisa Frisbie. *Moving Forward after Divorce.* Eugene, Or.: Harvest House, 2006. Print.

Manfred, Erica. *He's History, You're Not: Surviving Divorce after 40.* Guilford, Conn.: GPP Life, 2009. Print.

Wegscheider-Cruse, Sharon. *Life after Divorce: Create a New Beginning.* Deerfield Beach, Fla.: Health Communications, 1994. Print.

Mid-life Crisis

Conway, Jim. *Men in Midlife Crisis.* Colorado Springs,
Colo.: Chariot Victor Publ., 1997. Print.
Sheehy, Gail. *Passages: Predictable Crises of Adult
Life.* New York: Ballantine, 2006. Print.
Sher, Barbara. *It's Only Too Late If You Don't Start
Now: How to Create Your Second Life at Any Age.*
New York: Dell Trade Paperback, 1999. Print.

Saving a Marriage

Chapman, Gary D. *Hope for the Separated: Wounded
Marriages Can Be Healed.* Chicago: Moody, 2005.
Print.
Gray, John. *Men Are from Mars, Women Are from
Venus: The Classic Guide to Understanding the
Opposite Sex.* New York: HarperCollins, 2004.
Print.
Smalley, Gary, Greg Smalley and Deborah Smalley.
*Winning Your Wife Back Before It's Too Late: A
Game Plan for Reconciling Your Marriage.*
Nashville: Thomas Nelson, 1999. Print.